Celebrating the Male Mysteries

R.J. (Bob) Stewart is a Scottish author and composer with 25 books in print, translated into many languages worldwide. He works with myth, imagination, music, and the primal magical arts of inner change and vision. Bob has twenty years of experience in theatre, film, television, recording and touring as a performer, with several award winning productions.

For the last ten years he has concentrated mainly on writing and working with small groups in Europe and the USA, towards regenerating ancient traditions of inner transformation for practical modern use.

Celebrating the Male Mysteries

R J Stewart

Illustrated by Miranda Gray

ARCANIA

First Published 1991 by
Arcania Press
17 Union Passage, Bath BA1 1RE

Cover design by Jeni Liddle
Text design by Pica Publishing Services

Text processing by
Mentor DTP
Bruton, Somerset

British Library Cataloguing in Publication Data
Stewart, R. J. (Robert J.) *1949-*
Celebrating the male mysteries.
1. Men. Psychology
I. Title
154.2081

ISBN 1-873596-01-4

The cover illustration is 'Earth God' by Chesca Potter, based on the Cerne Abbas Giant hill figure in Dorset, England

For information on signed, limited edition, hand-coloured linocuts of this illustration, write to:
Arcania Press
17 Union Passage, Bath
Avon, BA1 1RE

Printed and bound in Great Britain

CONTENTS

Author's Note to the Reader

This is a book on the Male Mysteries; I hope that both women and men will read it, but the practical developments and exercises are specifically for men. It restates primal male magic through techniques for transforming consciousness and energy such as are found in humanity's perennial wisdom traditions. There is a special emphasis upon our vast inheritance of such knowledge and techniques from western sources, including those of ancient Greece, the Celts, western magic and mysticism, and the wide range of primal and shamanistic techniques found all over the western world. It is not a historical book, but a practical one, and in Part Three offers an original and unique working programme of visualisation for men, which has not been previously published.

I would not wish to be superficially accused of proposing any kind of return to outmoded male-dominated customs of social, political, religious, or sexual hierarchy: much of this book is intent on demolishing such hierarchies, and showing how deeply they damage us all, men and women. The exercises and illustrations are however, specifically designed for and about men, involving male energies and male responses to images in visualisation. Thus there is an intentional absence of feminine aspects in some of the universal symbols used in the illustrations, such as the Wheel of Life, or the Tree of Life, in which emphasis has been given to the male aspects.

Anyone who has read my books over the last decade or so will know that they place a strong emphasis upon the feminine forces of the psyche (be they in a male or a female person) and upon the need for a continuing powerful revival of awareness of the Goddess. This awareness should be of nature, in humanity, of the universe itself, and without it we cannot reach balance, either individually or collectively. This book is a manual (no pun intended) for men who seek inner transformation, offering techniques that can lead to rapid and permanent results. There is however, both a specific and a running discussion of the relationship between modern men and the Goddess, and one of the deep levels of visualisation in the work programme involves powerful goddess images.

I intend to develop in two further books the subject of polarity working between woman and man (still crudely known as 'sexual magic', a much abused and misunderstood term), and the harmony of the Male and Female Mysteries. These books will deal in depth with practical work for groups, whereas this present volume deals in depth with individual visualisation and male energy and consciousness. So certain essential and important subjects are, quite intentionally, set aside in this book, as they will be given full development in their own right.

How to Use This Book

While writing this book, I have been aware of the difficulty that modern men have in working with inner matters, with the arts and disciplines of consciousness and energy. Not that we are incapable of doing so, but that many of us are unable to find what we think are the right personal or social circumstances to do so, and, of course, that simple information is lacking. While there is a huge range of books and classes on both spiritual and psychological matters, there is very little designed specifically for the man who seeks by inner means to transform and emerge into the future. Much of that specific knowledge has been denied to us by history. This situation is dealt with at length in the Introduction and following chapters of Part One, so I will take it no further here.

I am particularly interested in a way of development, yet to be established, by which the individual or a small group can work without feeling obliged to enter into existing movements, schools, societies, study groups, or any of the alternative mystical magical or psycho-therapeutic systems.

As the reader will soon discover, I feel that any way ahead has to come from a restatement and simple redevelopment of some of the primal male magic that has been hidden, suppressed, or perverted by vested interests over the centuries. Men have a habit of becoming over zealous when they join movements or religions; the warrior urge and the religious urge are not that far apart from one another, no matter how much we might intellectualise or wish otherwise. Joining often amplifies our weaknesses, and gives us attractive and seductive excuses not to truly examine our motives and our deepest inner needs.

The practical work in this book, therefore, is designed either for the man working alone, or for a small group, possibly beginning from little or no experience of meditation and visualisation. Having said this much, the exercises in Part Three are not simple tuition in such matters, they are powerful transformative tools, with many levels of possible effect. There are, of course, a vast number of handbooks on concentration and meditation, and some of these are listed in the Bibliography.

The key to development in the Male Mysteries is simple: calm regular work not *upon* but *within* one's self. The model of the Five Branches used in this book gives five categories of male energy and primal expression (Warrior, Poet, Priest, Prophet, King). All five are inherent in each of us, and have a further broad correlation to the human anatomy, subtle energies, and psyche. Their empowerment and unity is within ourselves, we are the primal man, the worker. As this simple fivefold model of male-being has resonances in us all, it is possible to develop exercises and visualisations which will work on progressively more powerful and transformative levels. In other words the inner exercises and visualisations do not progress from 'beginner' to 'advanced'; this is the type of concept and potential delusion that men need to rid themselves of, as it may imply meritocracy or divisive hierarchy.

A true hierarchy is a holism, in which all parts are integral to the whole and any part is, paradoxically perhaps, the whole. The Five Branches model works in this manner, and can be used by the man with no experience of inner arts and disciplines just as effectively as by one with years of training in visualisation and meditation. The reader who is already familiar with some basic modern psychology will notice that the Five Branches used in our various visualisations are not the mythic or family orientated archetypes or life-phases so frequently found in modern publication and therapy. In this book you will not find extensive discussion of the roles of Father, Lover, Son, such as are given in men's studies or groups, in psychology, and in revivals of esoteric or spiritual and magical arts today.

To a certain extent this non-emphasis upon such life-roles is organisational and intentional in the context of this book, simply to avoid confusion of methods and terminology. But upon a deeper level, the pattern of Five Branches used here, the male images and powers of Warrior, Poet, Prophet, Priest, and Primal Man or King, have within each of them the archetypes or roles of Father, Lover, Son, and of course, the unifying role of Brother. Thus the images or Branches may act and react as Companions or Brothers (a role which we concentrate upon in this method), Fathers, or Lovers, just as any man may act or find himself entering upon during his life-cycle.

The deeper visualisations of the Mysteries involve encounters with Goddesses, who act as Mothers, Lovers, and Sisters. In this type of work, drawn from ancient traditions of empowerment, it seems to be the Companion, Sister, or Brother images (or gods and goddesses) that are required for modern work, prior to our real encounters with the universal Mother and Father images and energies. I would propose that this is a reflection of our current social and spiritual condition, in which there is a considerable imbalance between our male and female energies and modes of consciousness, and in which the collective and individual images of the Father and Mother are, as any psychologist will tell us, frequently corrupted and confused.

In the mythology, religions and initiatory arts of the ancient world, however, we still find this role of the brother and sister deities specifically emphasised, and we see them acting to assist, enable, and transform humanity, In a purely male context, it is frequently the sister-goddesses who teach warrior and poet skills, inspire prophecy and priesthood, and both curse and bless certain heroes who epitomise humanity seeking to develop, transform, and become truly (rather than mechanistically) civilised.

Whatever is embodied in mythology may be activated through the imagination, and will resonate in each and every one of us, male or female, if we do so. To restate and reopen the Male Mysteries, we need at certain stages to explore and experience the mythic patterns and powers described briefly above. For more detailed work with such patterns and powers, I will leave you to explore the visualisations and experiences offered in our later chapters.

There is an old eastern saying that 'when two masters meet, they smile'. This has hidden depths. Initially it means that when two men well versed in their own spiritual traditions meet one another, there is joy and not antagonism between them. It also means recognition, the smile of recognition that comes when two men from traditions that may be culturally separated realise that they share the same experience, even though they have come to it by quite different routes. If you work well with the methods given in this book, you will eventually become liberated from any one tradition, religion, or set of beliefs, and will come to recognise power when you meet it. This can often be in subtle guises, power for good or ill.

The culmination of the exercises in the third part of this book involves powerful sequences of visualisation aligned to the Four Directions, of East, South, West, and North. Through the Mysteries, a man unifies the world within himself, and brings together all directions harmoniously. Before he can do this, however, he must also encounter the Goddess, the female forces of life and consciousness and the universe, both within himself and in whatever outer expressions She may take in his life. Without this essential realisation of the Goddess within, no man can find direction or begin to unify the Directions, and no society can be at peace either with itself or with others upon the planet.

The first last words of the Male Mysteries are that of the ancient encouragement, or some might say warning, written over the Temple: 'Man, know thyself'.

Introduction

The aim of this book is to present some insights and practical methods towards reinstating the Male Mysteries for the twenty-first century. The material presented is drawn mainly from perennial esoteric or magical traditions, utilising practical methods which enable the individual to attune afresh to ancient and specific mythic and transformative potencies. We shall be examining some of these potencies, in the forms of energies, images, experiences, and thresholds of inner transformation in our later chapters. Many of the concepts and techniques are radically re-examined in a modern context, and some new methods, proven by long practice, are included.

The traditions upon which these new appraisals and techniques are based, however, are the enduring wisdom traditions, particularly those of the western magical and transformative schools of development. The nature and purpose of these schools or streams of tuition and initiation will be discussed in several places in this book, for there are many inter-connected illusions and delusions, particularly in the realm of male spiritual development, that should and can be avoided.

What Are the Mysteries?

Throughout this book the word *Mysteries* is used repeatedly. It is worth briefly defining how the word is used in our text, for there are a number of different meanings found in modern literature, and a quite distinct historical and cultural meaning for the Ancient Mysteries of classical civilisation.

In the historical sense the Mysteries of the classical world were organisations that claimed to initiate members to levels of spiritual realisation beyond those of regular temple or folk religion or popular magical arts. They combined ceremony, imagery, fasting, meditation, instruction, and revelation. They were superseded by the growing religion of Christianity, and as formal organisations eventually vanished.

But a number of underground movements and traditions persisted right into the present century, in attenuated forms. These manifested in each century in different ways,and are often identified with certain religious movements, magical or initiatory orders and societies, and the perennial collective teachings found within primal or folk traditions in every land. While we cannot say that any one of these many examples is a true Mystery in the classical sense, they are all representative of The Mysteries in a timeless sense, for they all combine many aspects of consciousness-changing technique into certain formal groupings and traditions.

In this book the term Mysteries is used in the broadest possible context; it means any initiatory and instructional stream of consciousness with accessible methods. Such streams of consciousness may have outer members and meetings, or they may be accessed solely upon inner levels through meditation and visualisation. They all begin where materialism, psychology, formal religion and common superstition falter and diminish.

The methods, potencies, traditions, images, and archetypes, employed in the Male Mysteries are shared by human consciousness worldwide, but manifest in various specific forms according to culture, environment, genetics, and, of course, physical and metaphysical gender or sexual polarity. The entire subject of gender and consciousness has attracted increasing attention in recent years, yet much of this has been entirely divorced from the perennial traditions or wisdom teachings which, in their own remarkable way, deal extensively and profoundly with such matters.

Throughout this book we shall be discussing many topics relating to gender, and its physical and inner or metaphysical reflections, polarities, and potentials. There is a popular delusion that physical gender is 'unimportant' in spiritual matters, or that we should 'rise above' sexuality in or through meditation and other spiritual disciplines. This delusion is one of the most enervating and poisonous traps for the individual, male or female, seeking liberation or enlightenment. Without an understanding of polarity, which is, of course, sexuality, our inner development or true balance simply cannot be achieved.

The very word 'enlightenment' is dependent upon polarity, for we may not raise our consciousness at the expense of any 'lower' part of ourselves or of others. Darkness is as essential to true psychic and spiritual realisation as light may be.

So many stereotypes regarding males as light-bringers and women as dark waiting wombs are found in modern self-styled spiritual literature and tuition, that it is sometimes difficult to grasp that such concepts play very little part in the inner spiritual teachings of our world. The stereotypical roles derive from suppressive political religion, and though the originals from which they are corrupted are true and valid in themselves, such roles are only one fragment of a cycle of polarity, a fragment which can be extremely dangerous if taken out of its deeper context. Fortunately the spiritual and magical traditions worldwide have always shown how such cycles of polarity and balance arise, spin, and return to their mysterious Source. This cycle, or more accurately spiral of cycles, is reflected in the Mysteries of every man and woman.

During the middle part of the twentieth century, a powerful revival of the Women's Mysteries began, manifesting initially as a political movement. The feminist political movement, paradoxically perhaps, has some of its roots firmly in the convoluted esoteric and spiritual impetus of the Theosophical Society, whose great reformer Annie Besant worked unceasingly for womens' rights in the nineteenth and early twentieth centuries. Enthusiasm for this Victorian and Edwardian politico-spiritual movement should be carefully tempered with a clear awareness of its powerful elitist and potentially suppressive hidden concepts. As it set the scene for the current revival of interest in spiritual matters outside orthodox religion, we should briefly examine its role further.

The Theosophical Society, despite its many admirable achievements in the causes of womens rights, racial equality, anti-vivisection, and ,of course, the liberation of India from British rule, had a surprisingly wide range of negative undertones. Many of these undertones were prevalent in other esoteric teachings and magical orders of the period, and have persisted unbroken to the present day, often re-manifesting in the New Age movement. We shall touch upon such difficult and potentially suppressive streams of consciousness throughout this book, but for the moment need to state the primary ones briefly.

The Theosophical Society, and related but far less politically influential magical Orders such as the Hermetic Order of the Golden Dawn, placed a strong emphasis upon 'hidden Masters'. These were an elite of supposedly superhuman males, living in secret isolation and dictating the progress of the human race. To a certain extent this concept derives from a perennial teaching concerning innerworld or spiritual masters, who are said to exist in, and act or communicate from, other dimensions, and to relate to humanity in many varying but generally beneficial ways.

The suggestion that such teachers are almost exclusively male, and that they are, in fact, super-physical beings moving secretly among humanity and steering our 'evolution' is a subtle but powerful twist to an age-old original teaching, and has many negative ramifications.

Such concepts are anathema to spiritual development, to equality and harmony of the sexes, and to individual emotional and mental maturity. At the most juvenile level they can lead weak misguided men to assume that they are, or soon will be, such 'Masters' but this is only the most obvious and trivial result. More subtly they presuppose that humanity is little more than a series of manipulated races or, at best, a collective entity being steered by higher forces and specific (male) intelligences. The worst extremes of this type of esoteric teaching merge imperceptibly with racism and fascism, in which superior male immortals cultivate a racial elite at the expense of other 'non-Aryan' or supposedly lesser races.

Much of this negative dross has permeated through into certain modern or New Age cults and societies, also claiming tuition from 'channelled' sources, hidden Masters, and the advent of an elect or elite within the present or next century.

This range of suppressive conceptual structures derives in turn from the political programming of historical or exoteric Christianity, carefully devised to generate belief in an 'elect' abandoning or even hostile to 'the damned', and firmly based upon male superiority.

Nor should we assume that movements based upon eastern (or more usually, pseudo-eastern) religions operating in the West are free of this long-term pernicious suppressive programme; very often the veneer of eastern spirituality and the glamorous use of exotic words and half-understood practices, masks what is at root an essentially Judaeo-Christian outlook. The much abused and misunderstand concept of karma is a typical example of this, while the pseudo-scientific use of 'evolution' within esoteric, spiritual, and New Age teachings, be they eastern or western based, is another. We shall return to these subjects in our later pages, for both karma and evolution are central to the Male Mysteries, though not in the popularised and often perverted manner in which they are regularly presented today.

Clearly none of this suppressive monosexual elitism is adequate or desirable for the twenty-first century, and any man or woman seeking inner growth should be very cautious indeed of working with any movement or set of teachings that derives from such sources or suggests such ideas. The most dangerous concepts are often subtly hidden or cunningly disguised with several layers of camouflage, and are often only fully perceived through meditation and contemplation, rather than in a gross outer form, though such outer forms abound in the current expansive warm wet climate of consciousness.

In our present context of the Male Mysteries, men need to be particularly aware that many lines or streams of concepts, of imagery, involving hidden Masters and so-called spiritual evolution, are in fact linked to the negative suppressive shadow of *enlightenment*, a word widely used to loosely mean spiritual liberation. For many centuries this shadow has resonated and manifested through male-elitism, which damages men as much as it does women. We shall return to this subject in many places in the following pages, as it is one of the major problems that men must address if they are to recover a proper Mystery or process of true enlightenment for the coming century.

Light is defined and enabled by darkness, and this mutual state of polarised existence holds good throughout all worlds, states, conditions, and cycles of existence. A *shadow*, however, is cast by *all* entities or shapes within the light. Although we may not realise it, a shadow is defined and created only by light, while darkness absorbs it without distinction. There are no shadows in darkness: this is why the ancient Mysteries of Isis revealed the spiritual light of the Sun at Midnight, darkest of the dark, yet brilliant. We shall return to this important paradox again.

At this introductory stage, however, we need to consider briefly the existence of the converse or suppressive shadow of enlightenment, for it is not, and never has been, connected to the antagonistic dualism of 'good' and 'evil'. The inner traditions, regardless of gender, race or creed, all teach that evil is a projection, confusion, or agglutination, of misaligned universal energy, and not, as is so often propagandised within orthodox religions, an insoluble entity in conflict with spiritual qualities of goodness .

The shadow of male domination is a resonance, a feed-back

pattern of collective energies on many levels, ranging from physical through to psychic to metaphysical. If we are able to untangle and realign these corrupted self-perpetuating energies, we make them available as sources of power which enable wholeness. The wholeness referred to is not any mere psychological or therapeutic integration, but takes form within the *pleroma* or holism of the universe, mirrored through octaves or images such as the planet, the land, the harmony of races, and the individual human being, male or female.

The late Robert Graves suggested that the legend of Alexander the Great (epitome of the powerful male stereotype), cutting the Gordian knot, emblem of the convolutions and weavings of the Mother Goddess, marked an important cultural and spiritual transition.[2] Although Graves' writings have been used by modern pagans and followers of the Goddess in a manner which undoubtedly amused the poet himself, as his *White Goddess* is full of complex jests and satires, we can pursue this particular image further. It is, of course, one of the great classical historical legends, and did not originate with Graves or any single writer scholar or poet; like a number of mythic or legendary themes, the story of Alexander is full of emblems and images out of time, beyond yet rooted into history.

To amplify upon Graves' interpretation, we might consider that this event was one of the symbolic thresholds, in mythic terms, between the older cycle of collective humanity worshipping the Great Mother, and male-dominated individualistic humanity which sought to control through drastic divisive antagonist means that which should, in truth, remain whole.

Cutting a convoluted knot, which Alexander is said to have done to fulfil the prophecy that whoever loosed the Gordian knot would be a powerful emperor, does not untangle it. The two parts remain as halves of an unsolved problem, now further divided by the sword.

In a recent and paradoxical revolution of awareness, we have found that modern technology, one obvious example of divisive, antagonist streams of consciousness and energy manifesting into our world, has revealed to us its own devastating planetary effect. Through science turning against itself at last, as maturity begins to slowly dawn, we are collectively more aware of the terrible threshold upon which we stand - nothing less than the potential death of the planet as we know it. Even if we chop the knot or knots into the tiniest pieces, hacking away stereotypically and manfully and vigorously, we have still failed to untangle it. And besides, cutting a knot at one level merely disposes of that level, for its innermost and universal convolutions remain intact.

The advent of open, or at least theoretically open, access to and practice of paganism in the post-war period has led to a large revival of Goddess awareness and worship in western society. This shift of consciousness and revival of an ancient but by no means extinct form of worship or holistic world-view, has been enthusiastically taken up by both men and women.

Men, however, have not had much open opportunity to reassess the inner or spiritual transformative dimensions of male potential. These were originally represented by what may be broadly termed the Male Mysteries in ancient cultures, and no counterpart of such systems or organisations exists today. Psychology frequently lays claim to techniques of maturation and integration which seem, quite plausibly and often with adequate proof and examples from individual case histories, to provide a path of development suitable for men. The twentieth century outburst of radical feminine awareness and Goddess consciousness is indicative of the failure of psychological techniques to meet the true need and power of the female psyche, either individually or collectively. The same failure must now be discovered in the context of male initiation or inner development towards balance and full potential.

There is a considerable difference between a psychotherapeutic or psychological approach to male initiation and transformation, and that of the spiritual or magical traditions. Although psychology can find parallels between its own modern systems and those of the esoteric traditions, such parallels only reach to a limited horizon. Beyond that horizon, the esoteric traditions extend, while psychology and psychotherapy must, due to their inherently materialist and limited nature, go no further.

In the 1960s there was a deep undercurrent of political and collective transformation of consciousness for women, much of which continues to ferment through western society today. In the 1990s and 2000s this undercurrent touches men, initially from a psychotherapeutic standpoint, but ultimately as a re-evaluation and restatement of the inner magical and spiritual potentials of male entity. And beyond that, we must bring this potential out into the world at large, the world from which we can no longer artificially separate ourselves.

This book, however, does not take a psychological or anthropological approach, partly because these are represented in other publications and in practical work, but mainly because the perennial traditions of spiritual and magical transformation, available equally and without distinction to both women and men, have a wealth of material concerning male inner transformation, most of which has never been published or reassessed for modern use.

Towards a New Generation

During the 1970s and 1980s, a new generation of spiritual teachers for women has begun to arise. These women have often come through political feminism, but have attuned to spiritual traditions, bringing new possibilities of transformation for women in general. In many cases these new possibilities are restatements of native traditions, rooted in a deep collective stream of awareness that regenerates itself in every century.[3] Can there be a new generation of teachers for men?

Before we can begin a proper answer to such an important question we must, once again, dispose of the sweetness-and light brigade. Kindly men with golden auras who exude loving brotherhood may, temporarily, give us some inspiration during dark phases, but they themselves are often locked in a backwater from which they cannot or choose not to emerge. Traditionally the Male Mysteries, regardless of the culture in which they manifest or the form which they take, are just not that easy. Teachers in native or chthonic traditions however, are notorious for being strict, devious, remorseless, and unkind.

We should carefully distinguish between this significant tradition of teaching in a non-sentimental manner, using perennial methods which aim to cut through all trivia and bring a true transformation within the pupil, and mere crudity or cruelty.

The crude and cruel methods, perpetuated among men in barbaric ways even today, are founded upon ignorance. The ignorance of the male-superiority ethic, the ignorance of the military mind, and, slightly more subtle but no less vicious, the ignorance of the meritocracy. The hard methods of spiritual and magical teaching, by comparison, are based upon deeper levels of understanding and wisdom, and have quite different goals, goals which might be incomprehensible to the man locked into aggressive superiority. Only when a man is able to realise that such aggressive meritocratic aims are delusions, can he begin to truly mature.

For most of us this realisation is present as an inner unrest, sometimes vague and too-easily suppressed, but sometimes of such a demanding nature that it cannot be ignored. Suppressing and ignoring this realisation of delusion leads to mental imbalance , to a reinforcement of the very traits that are the cause of our dissatisfaction. The vicious aggressive male ultimately destroys himself, but can wreak terrible havoc upon others before he does so.

The transformations and realisations of the Mysteries are not only enabled by, but are actually embedded within, techniques that have endured for millennia, and have acquired a considerable collective energy and effect. We shall return to this concept from time to time throughout this book.

We have all heard the suggestion and excuse that cruelty by teachers or parents is practised 'for his (or their) own good'. Insecure bullying men have used this excuse for generations to allow themselves the thrill of imposing their will and physical strength upon younger men. This type of cruelty in training plays no part in the inner traditions. A wise teacher, though, may often seem to treat a pupil in a very harsh and uncompromising manner, in order to bring the pupil to a threshold of inner transformation. This does not ,at any time, involve imposition of will, and no one, male or female, can be forced into spiritual growth by another individual. The teacher may, and often does, create difficult situations or tasks which bring out the latent potential in the pupil. That is quite different to bullying.

If we are to develop a new generation of men, men who will be able to pass spiritual perception and balance on to others,men who will forego egocentric inflation for the sake of a future society of harmony, we need to challenge many of the preconceptions of male dominated pseudo-spirituality.

The wise elder is typical example of this problem. While many young men challenge and despise the false teachers of their childhood, those who imposed upon and indoctrinated them at school or college, very few of us challenge the root concept of the wise elder in its own right. We tend to accept that there must be (somewhere) older wiser men able and willing to teach young ones; indeed we tend to long for this type of teacher or leader, for not only is the delusion conditioned into us by our culture, but it plays heavily upon our weaknesses, our childish willingness to absolve ourselves of responsibility and to pass all serious matters onto the shoulders of another. Not for nothing have the world's most vicious dictators been hailed by their people as saviours, fathers, holy men.

The true situation regarding teaching is very different. We all, men and women equally, learn most from *interaction*. In ordinary life this is, hopefully, acquired through experience,and we may have to undergo many bitter personal experiences before such interaction truly changes us. Through inner work in meditation, visualisation, and other spiritual disciplines, we may dissolve the illusion of the wise old man, and come to accept each teacher, inner or outer, simply for the quality and intensity of interaction, exchange and, hopefully, transformation, that he or she might have to offer.

Some of the typical polarities and scenarios are well represented in the Mysteries, in mythology, in legend, and in esoteric training. Some are amply defined by modern materialist psychology, though there is a tendency in psychology to limit the material to a very narrow range or to preconditioned and predefined potential. During the 1989 Merlin Conference, held in London, an open debate was held, based upon a motion that modern materialist psychology had, effectively, stolen a fragment from the spiritual traditions known worldwide. Much of this debate is developed by a group of contributors in *Psychology and Spiritual Traditions* (Element Books, 1991), but as psychology is still a male dominated and male orientated field, it is worth some special attention in the context of the Male Mysteries.

First, we need to be truly aware that psychology, regardless of any particular school or movement, is merely a model or variety of models of the human psyche. It has no validity other than as a model, and the different schools of psychological theory and practice can and do disagree with one another. One of the problems of psychology is that it was developed almost exclusively by western males without reference to alternative world traditions which contain other models of the human psyche. Psychology has become an alternative to religion, an alternative to inner discipline and spiritual development. It has a difficult inheritance from the nineteenth century, when male intellectual giants were attempting to reach beyond religion and superstition, yet were doing so in a society which was utterly conditioned by male-dominated Christian habits, behaviour, beliefs, and attitudes of life. It was certainly a great achievement or failure of the bootstrap theory, depending on your point of view.

Students frequently cite C.G.Jung as being a bridge between spiritual traditions and materialist psychology, but his role is really that of an Autolycus, a snapper up of trifles. Fragments of eastern and western tradition have been loosely incorporated into Jungian, and then into post-Jungian psychology, often out of their proper life-context, merely because they are found to work in some respects, and can be fitted into the framework of the psychological system concerned. Those aspects of the same traditions that do not fit, however, are conveniently ignored. Modern psychologically based techniques now abound, many of them claiming to be heralds of a New Age, to be transpersonal, to restate spiritual truths for the modern man and woman.

If we look closely at these alternative therapies, they are often based upon a small number of very simple and effective techniques which originally formed a part, and only a part, of broader traditions of spiritual and magical transformation. Frequently the result of taking such fragments out of their deeper original context is that they can become sources of imbalance, addiction, temporary adjustment or even a cult-like pseudo-religious obsession.

Typical examples might be cited: primal screaming, rebirthing, encounter groups, psychosynthesis. These and other therapies all work, no one would deny their effect, but they are essentially fragments of techniques, either rediscovered in a vacuum, or deliberately borrowed from older traditions of transformation. Rebirthing, for example, is a very commercially orientated reworking of the extremely ancient birth and incubation techniques known to the classical and Celtic cultures.[4] Apart from this important but conveniently ignored connection to a fragment of the ancient temple techniques of past civilisations, rebirthing techniques are still practised today among primal peoples for spiritual and magical initiation. Note that they are used for tribal or family initiation, and not for commercial therapy.

Many of the highly praised or advertised effects of alternative therapies, and indeed of mainstream psychotherapy, are simply regarded within the magical and spiritual traditions as relatively minor results. In a modern commercial context the catharsis of rebirth or of sudden realisation is held to be an aim in itself; in the perennial traditions such events were merely part of a series of thresholds leading to inner transformation. They were never ends in themselves, merely side-effects or transitional stages through which the individual passed.

In more customary and conservative fields of materialist psychology, we find the typical Victorian concern for labelling. If something can be labelled, it need not be understood. A label also distances us from the subject matter; we need not be involved in it too deeply, we can stand aside and consider it coldly, dispassionately; when we find something that we do not understand, something that instils fear or doubt or uncertainty, we try to fit it to our set of labels. Thus archetypes, gods and goddesses, mythic patterns, and the flow of energy in the human psyche and body, are all reduced to a set of labels within a conceptual framework. We have a comfortable feeling, thereafter, of knowing what we are talking about, writing about, experiencing, or, perhaps, avoiding experiencing. Victorian psychology and occultism share this entrenched attitude.

Now it has to be said that the same concern with naming names is true of genuine ancient and contemporary magical and spiritual traditions; the Mysteries (in any form worldwide) are replete with systems, labels, connective structures and so forth. They do not, however, regard the system, the label, as being of any value in itself; there is no reductionism in the Mysteries unless the individual chooses, in a typical modern sense, to reach no further than the labels themselves.

This apparent similarity between mythic re-tellings and obsessive listings is brought into proper focus when we realise that the original mythic epics and magical correspondences were not written down, but were vehicles of a living oral tradition. The use of images and verses from memory rather than from the printed page is an essential aid to transformation of consciousness: this is why magical traditions insist on learning by heart what seems, to the modern intellect, to be a mass of superficially indigestible lore.

Much of our response to ancient mythic patterns and magical or religious systems is heavily conditioned by that same Victorian obsessive labelling as materialist psychology; it is most unlikely that the lists of correspondences used in the esoteric traditions were ever regarded as scientific or authoritative in the nineteenth century sense that still dominates much of modern thought and practice. They were more in the nature of incantations, dream flows, protean collections that were used to attune the consciousness to holisms, rather than to reduce perception to series of items.

The Male Mysteries, like any branch of esoteric tradition, are essentially practical. The male-dominated elitist secret societies and occult orders of, for example, the nineteenth century, tended towards the intellectual, the hierarchical, and of course towards extreme obscurity. But there are older traditions, sometimes hidden within intellectual occultism and sometimes quite separate from it. It is the hidden traditions that we should restore for the present day, and it is in those traditions that we find the direct teachings, myths and legends of the Five Branches, and their empowering gods and goddess forms.

In the second part of this book we will examine the Five Branches of Warrior, Poet, Prophet, Priest, and King, and their effect upon the Worker or Primal Man who is both the beginning and end of the Mystery. In the third part we will use exercises in meditation and imagination that put us into direct contact with the god and goddess forms that empower each Branch, and we will develop a set of simple but powerful methods of working with such images for individual and group transformation and empowerment.

Part One

~

The Male Mysteries, Ancient and Modern

~1~

The Gods Within/Without

Men and the God

So many confused, contradictory and interrelated assumptions are made concerning the relationship of men (by which we mean males rather than an outdated collective term for humankind) to the gods, the god, or God, that it is almost impossible to untangle the resulting complex mess. Nor should we need to do so, as much of it is already rotting away and, thankfully, being discarded. In our present context of the Male Mysteries we do not need to delve too deeply into the dogmatic assertions of formal religion; we are working instead upon a subtle or esoteric level that both transcends and underpins many aspects of religion, psychology, and inner or transpersonal development without necessarily confirming or rejecting any particular dogma or faith.

There is no suggestion here of elitism, merely that it is possible to learn directly from perennial educational initiatory traditions. Such wisdom traditions reveal the essentials behind magic, religion, and mythology. These essentials are simple, but they are often obscured by an accumulation of formal arts, sciences and religions in each century.

Modern developments of the Mysteries do not demand or require religious faith, but neither do they deny it. Most of the concepts and exercises in this book, for example, are of a practical and technical nature; they may be undertaken and carried out without conflicting with any basic religious belief. Obviously people with a selfish interest in retaining religious authority and power over others will object very strongly to this type of suggestion and approach; nevertheless this book, like the Mysteries and perennial teachings upon which it is based, is not designed to undermine or contradict faith or belief, or to be antagonistic to any specific stream of religion.

Of more concern, however, than any fruitless argument over the validity of dogma or faith, are the long term psychic and social effects of such dogma and of spiritual suppression. These long term effects have worked deeply upon both men and women, and on this collective and individual level clearly the relationship between males and the god is in a very sorry state indeed.

Nor has modern psychology been helpful to us, especially those branches of Jungian and post-Jungian psychology which seem to take a great interest in mythology and perennial imagery. Although some schools of psychology are considered to be amicable and even helpful towards spiritual realisation, they may ultimately be more pernicious and destructive or negative in effect than the excesses of behaviourism or hard-line Freudian theory and practice, both of which, at least, leave the perennial traditions alone. Jungian, post-Jungian, and transpersonal psychology is all too frequently limited to those segments of ancient wisdom, magic, and mythology which fit psychological theory, while blandly discarding or ignoring those (comprising by far the greater part of the perennial body of lore) which do not.

Much emphasis has been placed by such schools of psychology and psychotherapy upon masculine and feminine qualities of the psyche, which are reputed to make themselves known through archetypes or god-forms as defined in ancient myth. These so-called archetypes (for the word is regularly misused in psychology) are assumed to be fragments or resonances of either a collective or an individual psychic state, as aspects of consciousness. But they are not considered to be aspects of any ubiquitous transcendent, universal consciousness, or, for want of a better term, divine Being. In other words, when psychology deals with the gods, they do not exist in their own right, they have no relationship to any universal holism or existence beyond the human psyche.

There are many subtle implications to this type of psychological theory, not the least of which is that any empowering concept or potential experience of either God or Goddess is constantly undermined by suggestions that it is nothing more than the projection of a simple psychic construct, psychological archetype, or sub-personality. Nothing could be further from the ancient concept of the goddesses or gods.

Despite the imbalancing and corrupting effect of political Christianity upon human culture and inner or spiritual development, it is only fair to say that such psychological reductionism has no role in orthodox religion. The strength of any formal religion, eastern or western (Christianity is, of course, an eastern religion grafted by force of arms upon the west) lies in its insistence upon a realm of Being that transcends, underpins and encompasses all others. The weaknesses that seem inevitable to political orthodox religion develop when the original spiritual insights and impetus become warped or corrupted into rigid law or dogma and eventually lead to persecution for political ends.

The God Within and Without

We need not focus this discussion upon religious faith, but can look instead to fundamental concepts which do not, nowadays, interfere with religion, mainly because they do not occur in the teachings of formal religion. More simply we may begin by considering *the god within*. What is this notion of a divinity inherent in humanity? Why do we feel, through all ages and cultures, that there is something inherent in every man that pertains to a god or gods, and in every woman that pertains to a goddess or goddesses?

In the Male Mysteries, one of the major empowering techniques and experiences, is to realise the presence of the god-within, and of the god-without. There is an unfortunate tendency for the concept of the god-without to be used for religious suppression of individual freedom, and for the concept of the god-within to lead to egotistic inflation and, in some cases, to the extreme evils of scientific materialism, the abuse of life, and the destruction of the land.

As we have discovered in the late twentieth century, the egomania of materialist science, striving ever onwards and seeking to wrest secrets from nature, linked to a profit-motive where anything is allowable to 'turn a dollar', seems to be leading to the wasting of the planet.

We might not think such gross imbalances and obsessions are to be related to the god-within...but materialist indifference and arrogance is part of that awareness of potential divinity; we behave like ego-maniac infants with powerful toys, knowing at last that there is no chiding deity to punish us for our so-called sins. Materialism is the direct inheritor of Christianity, which was the one religion that declared nature not to be sacred, but to be evil and therefore legitimate to abuse. This justification of the abuse of nature and all other entities, including non-Christian humans, is at both the heart of orthodox Christianity, and at the heart of materialism and science.

We are not, however, solely concerned here with these negative manifestations of concepts, but rather to seek a balanced insight into the most simple roots and energies that comprise the relationship between a male human and the empowering entity or energy of a god. At this stage it is irrelevant what name, kind, type, or origin the god may or may not have.

If we were to strip the entire subject of both religious and psychological jargon, we would find a very simple set of concepts, a situation which can be accepted or rejected. If we accept these concepts, or, more important, if our intuition and meditations confirm that there is truth in them, they act not only as a foundation for establishing parameters of consciousness and energy but as initiatory thresholds towards inner change. This is what the Male Mysteries, and indeed any Mystery or structured system of self-revelation and inner change, are all about.

Gender and Polarity

The male entity, defined very generally, but not exclusively, by gender, is the human biological equivalent of a universal relatively male or positive polarity. The female entity is relatively negative in polarity.

By the terms positive and negative, we emphatically must not imply good and bad, or any illusory fixed value whatsoever, but should simply define relative polarities of energy. These polarities cause movements of energy and form, which arise, cycle, and transform, through an infinite number of states or conditions in our universe. The relative divisions or interactions are simply a property of consciousness in time, our way of filtering the holism into smaller archetypes or sub-sets that we can relate to. In altered consciousness, different from our habitual or conditioned state, different resonances or octaves of the universal holism are perceived.

In the human physical body our sexual definition is that of the penis and vagina, (the first being physically outreaching, the second being physically receptive). But upon inner levels of energy we find that the male is sexually negative or receptive, while the female is sexually positive or outreaching: the polarity cycle is ever-spiralling. This teaching has been known for thousands of years in magical arts, yet has been heavily suppressed by orthodox religion and related social and political expressions in our culture. It lies at the very heart of sexual or polarity magic in which energies are exchanged, transformed, and greatly amplified through the flow between the alternative polarities of the humans working the magic, visualisation, or ceremonial pattern.

Esoteric tradition uses a number of simple but profound conceptual models to show this subject of cyclic polarity, and to relate them within a holism that ultimately resonates through all Being. Typical examples of such models are shown in our Figures 1 and 2 (pp. 8-11), the Wheel of Life and the Tree of Life.

The basic condition of being male, which is defined by, but not limited to, physical gender, means that when various life-energies manifest upon the physical level, they tend towards a positive or male polarity. Upon inner levels, which are reached through imagination, visualisation, meditation, and (less frequently but very effectively) through ritual or ceremonial patterns, the polarity or energy flow will change many times. Each threshold or change reflects an inverse: that which was immediately male upon the physical level becomes female inwardly: cross another inner threshold and it becomes male again. Much of this sequence is shown in our Figure 3 (pp. 12-13).

Energy works through a universal 'law' or tendency of octaves, by which the same pattern reiterates itself upon levels or rates that are octaves of one another.[4] Thus a male body has a powerful octave of male polarity, and this is what we might justifiably call the god-within. Between the outer habitual male form and the inner power, are various harmonic levels of energy and polarity.

The Three Aspects of Man or God

Let us consider briefly a situation in which a man seeks to realise the god-within. In other words, a male meditates, invokes, and visualises, seeking to build a bridge between his outer mask or personality, and his inner octave of universal male energy. This type of exercise has been undertaken by men for millenia, though the methods and forms vary according to religious, cultural, and environmental factors. Certain constants or archetypes permeate all systems and examples, and we may consider these before progressing to any actual visualisations or bridge-building exercises for the modern man.

In psychology, as we have mentioned, classical god-forms are often borrowed either as working archetypes or as analogous examples for temporary identification or 'explanation' in therapy.[5] Thus we have the obvious patterns of a god of war, a god of wisdom,

Figure 1 - The Wheel of Life

The Wheel of Life is a map, glyph, or mandala showing four fundamental relative states of energy, consciousness, and being. They interact as four ideal Elements of AIR/FIRE/WATER/EARTH, and as the Four Seasons of SPRING/ SUMMER/AUTUMN/WINTER. In meditational work they are aligned to Sacred Space (see Figure 10), the Four Directions of EAST/SOUTH/WEST/ NORTH, and the Quarters of the day, DAWN/NOON/EVENING /NIGHT. Work within this fourfold pattern leads to harmony, relatedness, balance and rhythm.

Our life-phases of CHILDHOOD/ADULTHOOD/MATURITY/AGE reflect the Quarters of the wheel or compass, with further rhythmic connections to the Lunar cycle of Waxing, Full, Waning, and Dark Moons (see Figure 7). The relative fourfold cycle is inherent in every energy pattern, every being. If we work from the still centre of the Wheel rather than repeatedly spin around it, we enter into a deeper understanding and conscious realisation of all aspects of the Four Quarters.

In the Male Mysteries, this consciousness is embodied as Four Companions the Warrior, Poet, Priest, *and* Prophet, *who stand at the intersections of the Quarters, Elements, and Seasons. They are inherent in every man, but are brought into consciousness through meditation, visualisation, movement, and rhythmic work within the Fourfold Circle.*

The flat pattern of the Wheel or Circle is really a map of our spherical *field of energy/consciousness. It is completed and brought alive by a human being in its centre, through the Directions of Above, Within, and Below. This is shown in Figure 10, defining Sacred Space.*

The Wheel of Life is also the ground plan for the primal universe, perfect world, idealised state, spiritual city, and the balanced sacred land. Such fourfold zones were frequently used in ancient cultures to attune the physical land, bringing a deep sense of relatedness and cyclic energy between humans and the environment.

1 = Childhood/Dawn (0-20 years)
2 = Adulthood/Mid-day (20-40 years)
3 = Maturity/Evening (40-60 years)
4 = Age/Night (60-80 years)
5 = Centre of Being (timeless present)

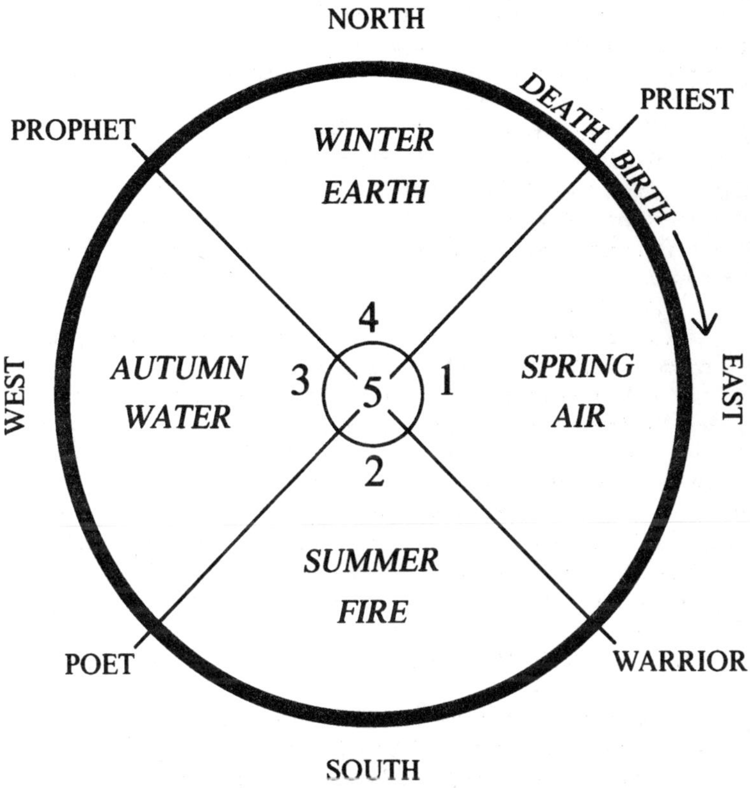
NORTH
PRIEST
PROPHET
DEATH
BIRTH
WINTER
EARTH
4
WEST
AUTUMN
WATER
3
5
1
SPRING
AIR
EAST
2
SUMMER
FIRE
POET
WARRIOR
SOUTH

Figure 2 - The Tree of Life

The Tree of Life is a traditional image combining human, planetary, mythic, and energetic attributes into a harmonious structure. It is used in various presentations in meditation and visualisation, and has a close correspondence to the energy centres of the human body.

The Tree or Axis Mundi (World Pillar) grows in the centre of the Wheel or Sphere of Life (see Figure 1). This empowers our perception of Sacred Space with an idealised model of the cosmos. The universal image of the Tree comprises Earth, Moon, Sun, and Stars as a central pivot, the planets and stars as polarised energies to the right and left, and the relative directions of the universe defined as Four Powers inherent in all being: LIFE/LIGHT/LOVE/LAW, (E.S.W.N.).

Ultimately, the Tree of Life and the standing human, the individual at the centre of the Circle or Wheel, are unified. In the Male Mysteries this is the realisation and manifestation of inner balance or Kingship (see Figure 6).

The Tree of Life comprises three triads or reflections of polarised male/female energy, each having a correspondence to the human body which reflects universal patterns and energies within itself. The first triad is stellar or universal, the second is solar or planetary, while the third is lunar and of our planet Earth. These are frequently shown in three concentric circles (see Figures 2a and 2b). The ten polarised spheres of the Tree are:

1. *Crown (of head): Primum Mobile or originative universal Being. Inspiration, breath, passes out and in through the throat.*
2. *Wisdom (left shoulder): The Zodiac or stellar wheel. Stellar gods, or the Star Father.*
3. *Understanding (right shoulder): Saturn. The Great Mother.*
4. *Compassion (left arm and side): Jupiter. Powers of Giving or creation.*
5. *Severity (right arm and side): Mars. Powers of Taking or destruction.*
6. *Harmony (centre/heart): Sun. Powers of balance, centrality, beauty.*
7. *Victory (left): Venus. Emotions or soul.*
8. *Honour (right): Mercury. Thoughts or mind.*
9. *Foundation (centre/genitals): Sexual and fertility powers.*
10. *Kingdom (feet): Matter, the manifest body, powers of the sacred land and planet.*

Polarity Patterns: The energies of 1/6/9/10 are central and bisexual, 2/4/8 tend to be embodied by male beings or deities, 3/5/7 tend to be embodied by female beings or deities. It is possible to define variants of the Tree of Life that emphasise either gods or goddesses in mythic terms (see pages 109-110 for god-forms upon the Tree of life).

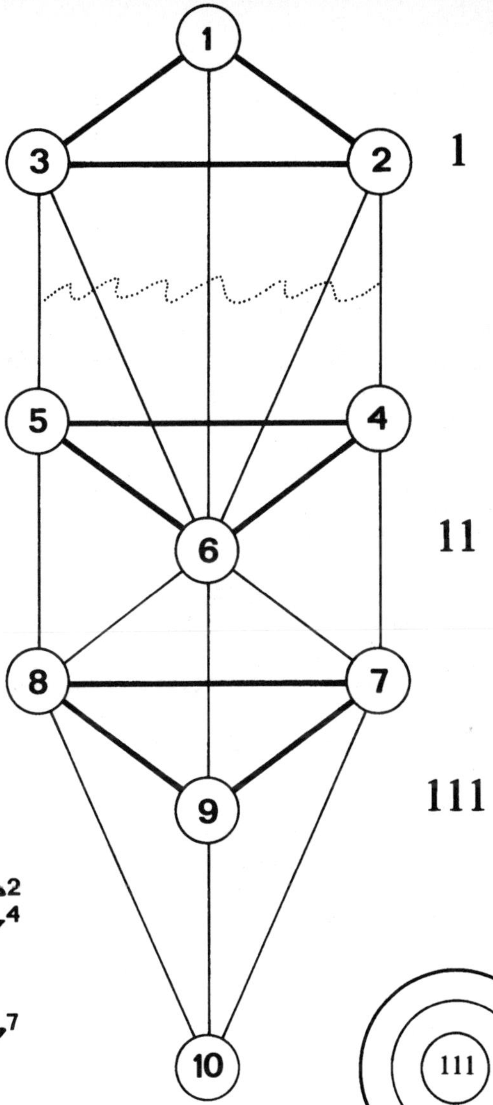

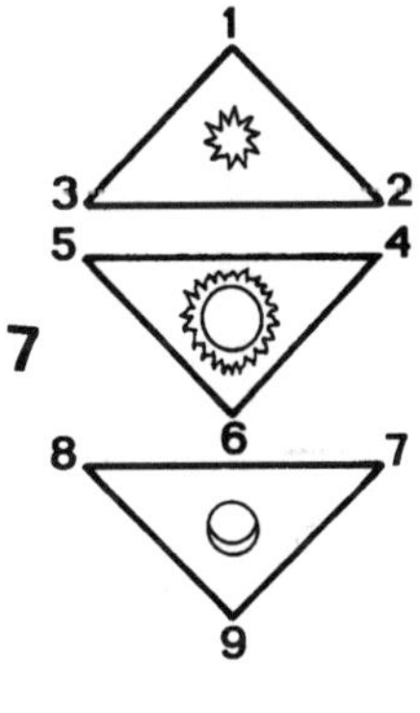

2a

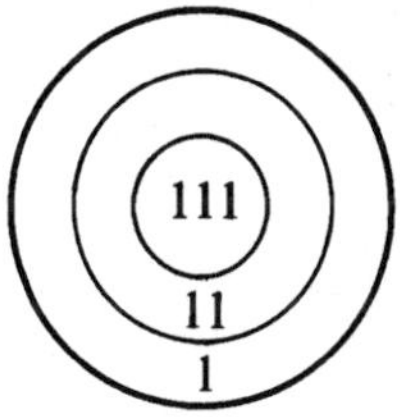

1 = STELLAR
11 = SOLAR
111 = LUNAR

2b

Figure 3 - Polarity Thresholds

All human beings are bisexual or potentially balanced and androgynous, regardless of physical sexual definition. Many of the stereotypes of masculinity and femininity vanish in meditation and visualisation with the discovery that gender does not define consciousness. Three main thresholds are often found in meditation or conscious work with inner energies and at each threshold there is an initial reversal of polarity:

1. *Outward male body*/1st threshold of sexuality/*inner female energies. Repolarises as male prior to:*

2. 2nd threshold of thought and emotions *(mind and soul)/repolarised male sexuality/inner female energies. Repolarises as male prior to:*

3. 3rd threshold of transpersonal or spiritual being/*repolarised male mind and soul (thoughts and emotions)/inner female energies. Inwardly female spiritual polarity to outwardly male body.*

Within all such thresholds and polarisations is the still centre or potential being which is balanced and androgynous. When we direct our attention inwards we cross the three thresholds towards this state of being. When our energies manifest outwards they define the three thresholds from an inner state of potential or androgynous being.

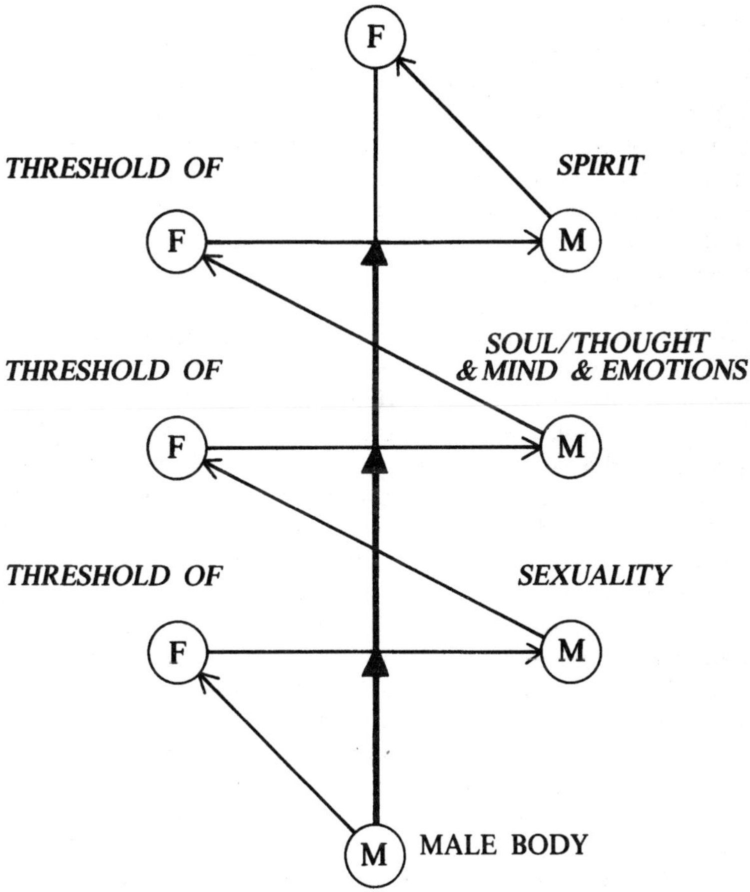
F
THRESHOLD OF
SPIRIT
F
M
THRESHOLD OF
SOUL/THOUGHT
& MIND & EMOTIONS
F
M
THRESHOLD OF
SEXUALITY
F
M
M
MALE BODY

and a god of healing, and so forth, which are supposed to represent archetypes or to be present as 'sub-personalities' in the human psyche. This is all reasonable as far as it goes, which is not, in terms of esoteric psychology, very far at all. The initiatory traditions certainly recognised the god-forms and used them extensively for practical work, but in a quite different way to their use in modern psychological and alternative, or New Age, methods of therapy or inner development.

One of the major differences is that the apparent family relationships inherent in the pantheons, much discussed in modern publications and emphasised in therapy, were relatively unimportant. Modern researchers spend an inordinate amount of time and energy defining pantheons and sets of gods and goddesses, comparing them to one another and showing how their relationships and mythic adventures are reflected in the modern psyche in interpersonal situations.

When such deities were actually worshipped and encountered consciously, they were of a far more complex nature than is evident in modern interpretation and reductions. The ancients knew perfectly well that each god or goddess has within his or her image many levels and aspects...there is no fixed, unchanging god or goddess in the pantheons of any culture. Upon a deeply mystical or philosophical level, we ultimately find the concept of One Being, but not as any kind of deity with an image, such as was used in ritual or visualisation to act as an archetype or focus between humans and the forces of the land, planet, solar systems, or stars.

In the Mysteries initiates were taught that the deities themselves went through the cycle of the Wheel of Life, and that they had changing aspects or relations with one another which were not publicly declared in state worship. In the case of a god, or gods, the *roles* of warrior, lover, father, healer and so forth, were of less importance than the underlying *aspects* or *phases*. The Three Aspects, Phases or Faces are as follows: Youth/Man/Ancient. (See Figure 4, pp. 16-17.)

This might seem to be merely a matter of chronology, and it certainly has its parallel in the human life cycle, but the Three Faces of a god (any god) tend to relate harmonically, or holistically, to certain properties and energies of consciousness: bright prophetic child or youth/wild or mad adult man/wise and experienced ancient.

If we take Apollo as a typical example of these three phases, the stereotypical classical Apollo, god of mental discipline, music, and intellect, is very likely be a modern (Victorian or post-Victorian) reduction. If we look at the myths and geomantic locations of Apollo, and of his Celtic manifestation Mabon, and the prophet Merlin, we find a quite different pattern, relating to the Three Aspects described above.[1]

Finding the God Within

As we have already suggested, the god may be found within or without. The god without has, for about 1500 years, been somewhat severely limited to a monosexual and imbalanced image, the 'demon Jehovah' (as William Blake described it) the wrathful father, the creator of pain suffering, inequality, restriction, elitism, misery, and so forth. This terrible image has been mitigated slightly by the that of Jesus, but suffering and pain are also features of this divine son in most orthodox Christian cults or religious branches. The problem of rivalry and pain between father and son, or older and younger males, seems epitomised in the formal religions, particularly those of near-Eastern origin such as Christianity.

This unfortunate and destructive historical pattern, (in which corruption of a mythic father/son divine pattern has heavily influenced human historical development, undermining the collective psyche and creating conditions of imbalance and effective evil) cannot be simply undone, even today after the virtual collapse of orthodox Christianity as a force in our world.

A man seeking the god-without, outside himself, can still take the orthodox religious route, but it is fraught with terrible barriers and suppressive imagery. To reach the true level of divine love and compassion that was originally embodied within Jesus, a man may have to work his way through the entire ambience and collective imagery and forces of orthodox religion. He may well lose sight of his original goal *en route*, or, as is more likely nowadays, simply realise that a corrupt and defunct religion is not worth his life energy. The failure of Christianity to meet the needs of modern people means that many individuals are lost, seeking a religious focus, but failing to find one. Too often the active cults of Christianity that seek recruits are of such a repellent nature, clearly lacking compassion or any type of wisdom, that many people are unable to accept what little they have to offer.

What are the ways in which a man finds the essential Being, the power, the divinity, within himself? In Chapter 3 we discuss some of the ways of action, skills and craft, and balanced living which act as outlets or routes for the energy of life, as it is expressed

Figure 4 - The Three Faces (Youth, Man, Ancient)

Another way of relating male energies and images to the Four Elements, Directions, and life-cycle, is through a triple pattern. This is frequently found in mythic images of gods and goddesses throughout the world. Any god or goddess image or archetype may appear in any of the three phases, youthful, adult, ancient.

A full cycle around the Wheel of Life (see Figure 1) will generate twelve images, god-forms, or archetypes. These may be embodied as mythic beings or as constructs within the psyche appearing in dreams, waking images, and as spontaneous figures arising in visualisation. They may also arise in primal or shamanistic arts as ancestral beings, which will often occur in triple presentation, with different implications or teachings according to the phase of youth, man, or ancient.

The triads of Figure 2 and the cyclic and five-fold shapes of Figures 5 and 6 may be related to this triangular shape in meditation. The pentagonal shape of Figure 8 is derived from the heart of a hexagram, formed of two intersecting balanced triangles aligned to the Four Directions. These simple properties of shape and relative energies have powerful transformative effects when they are used in techniques of empowerment through meditation and visualisation. They also play a major part in sacred dance or ritual pattern making, in which movements of our bodies in a defined space reiterate the energies and patterns of Sacred Space, of the universe.

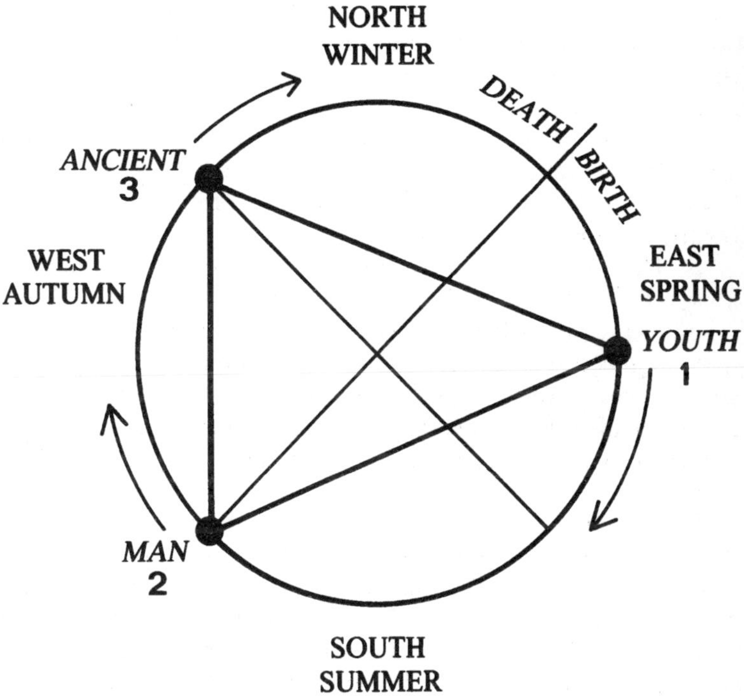
NORTH
WINTER
DEATH
BIRTH
ANCIENT
3
WEST
AUTUMN
EAST
SPRING
YOUTH
1
MAN
2
SOUTH
SUMMER

through a male entity. These are not a complete catalogue or so-called 'authoritative' list, merely some indications from spiritual and magical teachings that persist through the ages.

The entire issue of finding the god-within, or the essence of our being, is related to sexuality. For most men the usual route is to work with a generally male self-image; that image is then modified and rapidly abandoned as the temporary mask that it truly is. But what does it mask - energy, life-force, and beyond, or within that energy an entity or Being that is more than ourselves? In terms of our own consciousness, even when it is beyond the delusion of a rigid 'self', this higher or transpersonal entity, this being, is still male.

At the most profound levels of meditation, such sexual identification vanishes, and the essence of Being is known to be bisexual, transcending, yet totally present within all sexuality, all polarity, all time, space, and energy.

The further we reach inside ourselves through meditation, the less defined sexual polarity becomes. In other words we do not intentionally pass within in meditation to be confronted by some male fragment of ourselves: we pass beyond any such relatively surface levels, and seek directly for the deeper roots of our being...this seeking will often, in itself, rebalance fragmented and habitual tendencies towards exaggerated stereotypical habits and behaviour.

Many men are afraid, even terrified, of any type of inward-looking meditation. They tend to confuse it, initially, with self-examination or moody introspection. We may set aside, for the moment, obsessive self-examination, or ego-mirroring and self-reassuring reveries and daydreams...these are not meditation, not true visualisation, and they do not reach beyond the more superficial levels of the psyche . In some individuals we find a highly energised loop of self-mirroring fantasies, such as perpetual self-examination, dwelling upon one's own thoughts, emotions, motives, decisions, and so forth. Modern psychology tends to reinforce this type of potentially pollutant self-examination by giving it an intellectual system.

Another typical and widespread self-mirroring fantasy that rules the lives of many men is the delusion of the man's man, the praiseworthy phallic achieving male. In Britain, the Medallion Man, who looks in every mirror, wears his shirts open to his navel to reveal his medallion, has become a figure of popular comedy, in recent years. And let us be honest at this point, we have all behaved like medallion-men. This type of self-image runs through most male activities and occupations; many men have little concept of what they truly are, who they are, relying instead upon a mirror built of stereotypes of pseudo-manliness.

The god-within is not a type of phallic super-male, nor is it the function of the god-within to release energies to enable us to behave in a manner that amplifies and encourages our current habits and delusions. One typical problem is that when men encounter the power within, either through an early meditational experience (for these early experiences can be very potent indeed), or through involuntary realisations (which come to all of us at least once in a lifetime), or through unusual highlighted or tragic circumstances which lead to a sudden change of consciousness, they tend to re-route the experience. By this we mean that men will channel temporarily increased energy through habitual traps and filters of the false personality.

The true experience of divinity or Being, therefore, becomes a source of temporary energy or buttressing for the deluded personality of the stereotypical male, for all our weaknesses and poisons. Many of the glowing, charismatic, wonderful teachers and gurus of male-dominated 'new spirituality' are simply individuals who have accessed a source of energy, but used it (consciously or unconsciously) to reinforce the self-delusion of male-wonderfulness. Too often the guru or New Age teacher is a type of psychically amplified Medallion Man.

We must remember that individual power is merely energy; if we do not have appropriate channels for it to flow through, it can only take what channels we have... in some cases a sudden access of true life-energy will destroy us, drive us mad. Traditionally, those who underwent the initiatory process became poets, madmen, or were found dead at dawn! These three conditions apply to us today...there are many dead men in all walks of life. We only need to think to realise how many we have met - how many madmen, but how few seers and poets.

In the third part of this book we describe and restate for modern use some of the perennial methods of obviating this problem, of realising the divine power within, but by using techniques which also breakdown and realign the rigid stereotypes of the personality. The forces of breaking, of change, are usually embodied within a certain type of goddess, the dark destroying figure who many men, and many women, most fear. This experience may come through bitter situations in outer life, or, more rarely, can be consciously faced and undertaken in inner work, through visualisation or ritual.

There is a wide range of potential parameters and combinations of energetic images and events, just as there is a seemingly infinite range of life-experience. In the old initiatory traditions, the method was always to work with a simple and limited pattern; this simplification and limitation, combined with intentional repetition, gave clear and well established channels through which energy could flow. In modern use, we find that a visualisation which employs traditional archetypes, god or goddess forms, scenarios, and patterns of narrative or events, may be repeated many times. Contrary to what we would expect from endless repeats of a popular entertainment, (which is that in most cases it would rapidly become tedious) repeated visualisation develops an increased level of energy, and many new realisations come through it. Additionally we should add that visualisers report that no two experiences of the same visualisation are ever identical.

2

Men and the Goddess

Just as it is impossible for women to truly realise balance and maturity without an open relationship with their inner male energies and psychic entities (the god within), so is it impossible for men to gain such realisations without their inner female energies and psychic entities (the goddess within). Modern materialist psychology has gone some way towards recognising and 'discovering' this truth, which was widely taught in the ancient Mysteries and still persists, often in rather obscure presentations, in the perennial esoteric traditions.

A degree of insight into the truth of the god- and goddess-within is only the first glimpse or reflection of a greater picture, for both men and women should also establish a proper relationship with, and within, the Great Goddess. She reflects through our inner energies, but She is a universal power and entity, a Being, underpinning, permeating, and transcending all other forms and forces.

No energy or space will be spent in this book discussing the existence of the Goddess; this is not a treatise on philosophy or religion. Exercises which include working with Goddess power will more than 'prove' her reality to even the most rigid and sceptical male, if he is prepared to work with them. The effects of such exercises, of course, will vary considerably, and some of the possible range of reactions will be outlined in various contexts throughout our text. As this is a book on the male potential for enablement and transformation through esoteric initiatory techniques, the range of reactions described is loosely confined to those found within men, but they mirror those of women in many ways.

None of the foregoing implies that all women have an inherent natural relationship with the Goddess, any more than it implies that all men have a natural relationship with the God. Many simply do not. One of the quite false assumptions in many modern publications and teachings is that sexual gender gives an individual some kind of spiritual entitlement...that women must, because of their gender, be in contact with the Goddess, and men with the God. This is a trap which runs through esoteric groups and magical orders today. It is really a type of subtle sexism, of gender stereotyping, and can cause real damage to spiritual development by placing unnecessary assumptions and expectations within the individual psyche.

It is worth noting in this context that in the pagan religions it was very common for women to mediate, invoke, and act as priestesses of gods, while men performed the same functions as priests of goddesses. One of the most dangerous and damaging delusions of the modern revival of Paganism and Goddess worship is that it has often fallen into the sexual stereotype trap of Christianity, but manifesting in a more subtle way. Because for many centuries no one had dared to say publicly that the Goddess lives within women, this statement is now assumed to be inevitably true, possibly through its shock value to those conditioned to patriarchal stereotypes of religion. We should remember also that it was generally heretical and punishable for men to state that God lived within them - God was always safely 'outside', usually upwards, and strictly regulated by dogma.

Magical groups and orders still perpetuate this sexual problem, in which only men are supposed to be able to mediate godforms or male energies, and only women to mediate goddesses. These suppositions are untrue; historically we may find many examples of polarity-working within sacerdotal and magical practices (i.e. males relating to goddesses and females to gods). This historical evidence is borne out very powerfully indeed in modern experience and practice of magical arts and esoteric techniques. Many men are deeply shocked by the suggestion that they can relate directly to the Goddess, or act as her priest - and little wonder after such a long period of deliberate suppression of this great truth.

In our context of the Male Mysteries we are concerned mainly with the transformative potential of the inner energies upon and through men, but it must always be emphasised that men and women are originally, ultimately, and potentially bisexual, and that a balanced humanity is one in which women and men are equal. A number of myths and legends demonstrate this truth.

In our current state of human development, balance may occur through male-female partnerships, but this important archetypical concept has been perverted and corrupted by the dogma of religion, and further degraded by the stereotypes of our society. The potential of equality and balance, however, remains. It is often found upon non-physical sexual levels, and much confusion and emotional disablement arises when men confuse inner partnership with emotional or sexual attraction.

The root of this type of problem, increasingly common as more and more people turn to inner disciplines and practices is that the general expectations of emotional relationships are widely at variance with the reality of our inner situation. One of the potential weaknesses and damaging aspects of modern psychology is it simply does not address the deeper levels of polarity or spiritual sexuality, and can often work against the true inner nature of the individual undertaking therapy. Such enduring and widespread confusion over the emotions and sexual polarities is one of the true victories of the suppressive long-term programmes seeded into human culture by manipulators of religion, for it destroys our potential for liberation, and amplifies imbalance and antagonism between men and women.

We shall return to this major subject in several respects, and in a number of variant forms and situations, as it arises in the context of the Five Branches of the Male Mysteries. It must also be stated at this point in the discussion that spiritual balance may also be realised by physical sexual means, through the exchange of energies between entities right through to the physical sexual exchange between human bodies. Despite all the well publicised pernicious stereotypes, these energy-exchanging bodies do not have to be rigidly confined to one-to-one male/female sexuality. There is a virtually lost scientific art of sexual magic which is gradually reappearing and reforming in our world.

Sexual magic is strongly represented in eastern cultures by Tantra, though there is so much popular misunderstanding and confusion over tantric practices (widely commercialised in Western literature) that extreme caution needs to be exercised. Many people think that simply identifying a sexual practice as 'tantric' brings it within their understanding or somehow justifies its use: this is nonsense. Without a deeper tradition, and without spiritual instruction and comprehension, special sexual practices are often pointless, and may even be negative, addictive, or dangerous.

The concept of sexual equality applies as much to the woman within man and the man within woman, as it does upon any interpersonal or other social or political level. We need to be very cautious, however, when dealing with those religious, spiritual, magical, and psychological teachings and writings in which men 'transcend' sexuality and become suddenly spiritual and ethereally bisexual or, more usually and quite ridiculously, non-sexual. Such systems and practices are merely a subtle variation of the anti-feminine propaganda that runs through orthodox religion.

Men cannot use bootstrap techniques to gain spiritual sexual balance, such as progressive enlightenment within an all-male religion with an exclusively monosexual divinity. No one will deny that certain levels of insight and energy are accessible through such practices, but they are quite unsuitable for the present cycle of human development, and historically have caused profound misery and suppression of the masses for the spiritual and material benefit of the (usually male) few. We need to dispose of this type of unhealthy and destructive practice altogether.

On a more esoteric level of comment, it should be realised that there is a very great individual price to pay for monosexual exclusivist enlightenment: it is the inner equivalent of a force-fed growth, a plant that shoots up tall but rootless. The height is gained without foundation, and may be elevated and dizzy indeed, but the inevitable fall and decay occurs later. We need not concern ourselves too extensively with such metaphysical matters here, for we are dealing with practical methods by which the Male Mysteries might be regenerated, rather than any trans-temporal science of spiritual development and reincarnation. This science, however, does play a major role in the Sacred Kingship, which is discussed in Chapters 6 and 7.

Perceiving as She

There is a simple turn-about of awareness that has deeply transformative effects. In essence it merely consists of perceiving everything in the material or natural world as the body of a universal Goddess. This body is neither inert nor passive, but alive, conscious, and active. We may, at first, only comprehend the parts, but like the human body (which is a small reflection of the universal body) every part is alive, conscious, a cell partaking of the whole. If we intellectualise over this, discuss it, and compare it in detail to religious and magical levels , metaphysical dimensions or worlds, or abstract mathematical theories, we lose it. The turn-about of awareness is something which is done, rather than rationalised, agonised over, or written about. On paper it seems to be a crude trick of words, but the effect upon consciousness and upon our vital energies is profound.

This is not, incidentally, an invitation to a type of religious paganism or worship of matter: it can be worked as an ever-deepening change of attitude regardless of faith. The core of this change consists of regarding the natural world, from our own environment to the environment of the universe, as inherently feminine. Not stereotypically feminine, not the yielding passive earth of the capitalist profit-orientated polluter, plunderer or destroyer, not even the Earth Mother, though She is part of this holism. Those who are devout materialists can make such a change of awareness just as easily, possibly more easily, than those with some type of spiritual conviction or knowledge. The fact that it is a mental trick, an intentional change of attitude, in no way limits its remarkable effect.

For men this transformation of perception is one way of developing a gradual realisation of the Goddess; other ways, embedded within the wisdom traditions of the world, the Mysteries, are the cathartic and often devastating initiatory images of the dark Mother, the Death Goddess, the Warrior Sister, all of which are essential in the Male Mysteries. If we resist these natural universal forces, they eventually manifest through our outer lives. In the most obvious way, none of us can ignore physical death.

Mother and Lover

Although we live in a time-period when it seems that a revival of Goddess-awareness is genuinely and unavoidably occurring, we should be constantly alert to the pervasive presence of enervating stereotypes within this revival. In many examples, it seems only too clear that what people are reputedly reviving is a set of inflated artificial images, rather than a true relationship to the Goddess or to ancient but by no means defunct or inaccessible Goddess traditions. To grasp this problem, (the existence of which might be denied by many modern self-styled pagan men and women who claim a new awareness of the Goddess) we need to examine some of the popular notions concerning Goddess-nature. We shall concentrate particularly on the manifestation of these popular notions in the minds of men, but it must be remembered that any such difficult areas of emergence and changing awareness are shared by men and women, and are not by any means confined to physical gender.

One of the more obvious sources of confusion is that of materialist psychology, where lengthy and seemingly profound statements and theories have been developed concerning the relationship between individual psychic archetypes and the ancient gods and goddesses. Thus when a man identifies a sexual lover as a 'goddess' he may blandly assume, (or his therapist or counsellor may assume), that this is due to some so-called archetype of consciousness being attuned to or located upon the woman in question. It would seem that the Goddess has to be either a lover or a mother...and this nonsensical and quite superficial reductionism is shared by many modern revival pagans. If the Goddess is understood as merely a large version of the conditioned images within our own psyche, rather than the true situation, in which we are reflections of her universal Being, we have fallen back into the very trap from which Goddess-awareness is supposed to liberate us.

The regrettable converse of the explanatory and reductionist effect of psychology is that men's notions of the Goddess herself are limited to mere psychological stereotypes, both in terms of modern intellectual materialist theory, and in the sense that this theory derives directly from religious propaganda. Such propaganda suppressed the true images and functions of the Goddess with the advent of monosexual patriarchal Christianity. This style of religious hierarchical authoritarianism (refined but not invented by political Christianity) was, and is, as damaging to men as to women, though it may take some bitter experience before men truly realise this and understand the full extent of the damage done, quite intentionally, to them.

3

Teachers and Pupils

The Personal Teacher

Much emphasis has been placed upon the personal teacher or guru in modern systems of spiritual development. We can add to this the emphasis of psychotherapy upon the therapist, a role which mimics the concept of the spiritual guide and teacher without necessarily fulfilling its original functions. Some, but by no means all, of this emphasis can clearly be traced back to the underlying concept of 'The Masters', widely promoted by the Theosophical Society in the 19th century. Many modern ramifications depend strongly upon the cult of personality - the great teacher, leader, guru, savant, and so forth. In some cases the great one earns enormous sums of money, but more subtly he, or far less often, she, gains many more subtle benefits at the expense of pupils, patients, clients, or trainees.

What or who should the male seeking truth look for today? Does he need a direct personal guide or teacher as repeatedly emphasised in so many text books, courses or groups? Does the guru concept of the eastern cultures work successfully for a westerner? What does tradition, stripped of modern accretions or corruptions, tell us about the importance of a guide or teacher for inner development?

First we must be very aware that teachers or groups promoting systems of development, or therapy, or realisation, for large sums of money are not, by their very nature, suitable for our needs. No inner development can be bought: no true teacher will sell his or her teaching. What, we might ask, can we gain from a teacher who advertises and charges money? What can we gain from a teacher at all?

The short answer to these questions is not enlightenment, or empowerment, but skill. A teacher can help us develop very specific and easily recognisable skills, techniques, and disciplines.

Often these skills are of a physical nature, an art, a craft, physical disciplines such as movement, co-ordination and perception. There are complex and profound traditions of teaching physical skills with underlying spiritual benefits: perhaps the most obviously commercialised of these today are the martial arts of the East, but there are many other examples, some of which we shall discuss elsewhere in this book.

The tuition of physical skills may indeed be justifiably charged as professional services: but anyone charging money for the benefit of our souls, our psychic or spiritual welfare, or for other subtle matters should avoided. The saying attributed to Jesus of Nazareth in the New Testament still applies today, though its original political revolutionary significance is no longer pertinent: 'Render unto Caesar that which is Caesar's, and unto God that which is God's.' Today this wisdom applies to the changing of money for the much touted benefits of New Age gurus, therapies, channelings, and cult membership: if any such movements have a true spiritual quality, they will require little or no money. Each level or world has its own energy and medium of exchange: material tokens cannot purchase subtle gifts or benefits. But subtle symbols or exchanges certainly can be made. Much of the tuition of the Mystery schools concerns such exchanges.

If a good teacher can help us to acquire skills, which skills in turn help our inner development, we may, within reasonable limits, use such tuition as part of a spiritual or magical programme of development, without seeking teachers who claim to sell us enlightenment. The skills, after all, are worthy of development in themselves, and any truthful teacher of inner development will tell you that only if you live through the various skills and arts wholly and utterly will they really work upon deep levels. This is quite different from acquiring skills to inflate the ego, make money, or 'prove oneself'.

A man seeking enlightenment or some level of change within the broad spectrum of the Male Mysteries today could indeed benefit from the skills that a good teacher has to offer, but skills do not comprise actual change or initiation. Any initiation sold for money is invalid, and may be even dangerous or weakening. The traditional scenario of the pupil and teacher is much misrepresented and misunderstood, but a brief analysis and restatement of the esoteric tradition which underpins such relationships in both East and West would be as follows: The relationship between pupil and teacher in the inner Mysteries or magical and spiritual traditions is never limited to a one-to-one isolated situation. It always takes part within the broad framework of a tradition, Mystery, or school of development. Many such schools have long traditions and deep roots, manifesting in various forms in each century.

Thus when a teacher and pupil work together they are merely parts of a holism, an interrelated Mystery or structure of inner development. There is a common delusion that the teacher-pupil relationship is like that of father and son: this is extremely dangerous to assume, and has led to many emotional and spiritual problems. In modern therapy for men much emphasis seems to be placed upon loving and forgiving their fathers, transcending jealously, hatred, grief, pain, and so forth, particularly when those pains are focussed upon the father from real or assumed childhood experiences. This plays little or no part in the Mysteries, and each male should learn how to unfetter his love beyond self. This loving beyond self includes parents, relatives, clan, race, and ultimately all that is.

The pupil-teacher relationship should never be that of the kindly father and the developing reciprocating son: if it is on this level it simply cannot work. Some men pass themselves off as teachers or masters to benefit from the emotional pain of their pupils, drawing upon and feeding from the energies of loss and love that have been imbalanced or frustrated in the pupil's childhood or teenage years. This tendency is frequently found in psycho-therapists, New Age or commercial teachers and guides, psychic counsellors, and cult leaders (regardless of the branch of religion that the cult derives from). We need hardly say that it is not confined solely to males, but is found across the range of such relationships.

There are a few little known factors in the traditional teacher-pupil initiatory systems, which are worth disclosing and publishing, especially as they are often concealed by male initiates practising such techniques when they find pupils of their own.

The first, that of the span of tradition and its holism, is most important. The crude concept of a master and pupil working solely together is simply untrue: most of the work is done upon inner imaginative levels, or in other dimensions of consciousness and energy. Such levels of consciousness and energy involve many other entities: mythic, transhuman, spiritual, ancestral, even down to the genetic or collective level. Thus the image of the older and younger male working in isolation and the wisdom being handed on is nonsense. Just as no man is an island, no teacher and pupil ever truly work together in intimate isolation.

Second, and least discussed, is the concept of role transfers in initiation. Terms such as this have come to have an accepted meaning in materialist psychotherapy, but the dynamics and deeper level of this important reflection of energies have long been known in the esoteric traditions.

To simplify this theory and practice, we might express it as a typical example: A young man approaches a mature experienced teacher for initiation into the esoteric arts and disciplines, (regardless of any specific tradition or religion, many of which could be fitted to this typical scenario). The teacher agrees, and begins training the pupil. But immediately a little known factor begins to play a part: eventually the master and pupil will change roles: the pupil will in turn become a master. And so? Is this not supposed to be the point of studying and initiation, to become an adept or teacher? Not at all; the aim of inner development is spiritual maturity and enlightenment, mastery is a coincidental occurrence, and must ultimately be disposed of. How do we dispose of it? By passing it on a pupil, who will in turn pass it on to another pupil, and so on.

So many men are desperate to acquire the mantle of their teacher, but only the initiate knows what this mantle is. It is the accumulated burden or karma of a long line of initiates, which is realigned with every wearer, and passed on to the willing pupil. The teacher is left free of this mantle at death, or in rarer cases, during a lifetime. The pupil takes it willingly, knowing that the burden will eventually pass from him to another. Originally this was a valid and good system: in early cultures it worked well, for each initiate took on a burden of responsibility from within the Order or Mystery, and carried it and attempted to resolve it through work in the inner and outer worlds.

Initiatory techniques still found in esoteric or magical development today can, and often do, pass on such karmic burdens to unwitting pupils. Unscrupulous adepts will try repeatedly to pass their karmic burden to younger pupils, but usually fail to do so. This is one of the typical loose ends and problems of male initiation in the modern era, a hangover from ancient times which has never been properly erased, discussed, or balanced. This problem of the Mantle does not, interestingly, apply to women, who inherit or gain a different kind of responsibility at initiation. Once again the difference is defined by the physical entity, the gender, and not by inner qualities, skills or levels of development. It is, essentially, one of the differences between fatherhood and motherhood.

Working With Innerworld Teachers

One of the proven methods of inner or transpersonal development, is through working with metaphysical teachers. The word metaphysical is used quite deliberately here, in its proper sense: in the Male Mysteries it is possible to learn from and work with entities that are not physical, but nevertheless have true existence in other states or dimensions. In this chapter we shall consider briefly what such states, dimensions and entities truly are. The technique is a very ancient magical one, found in all perennial wisdom traditions and religions world-wide. When we apply it specifically to male development, however, certain clear parameters appear, and certain very specific innerworld teachers, adepts, and mythic or divine entities are emphasised. While many of these entities are masculine, some of the major figures are feminine. This is such an important matter that it needs to be repeatedly affirmed: some of the major transforming and enabling entities found in the initiations of the Male Mysteries are feminine. Without these figures, archetypes, entities, or goddesses (call them what we will) no man can possibly develop: just as he could not have been conceived and brought to birth without a physical mother.

But we need not assume for one moment that such feminine figures in the Male Mysteries are motherly; many are quite unmotherly and terrifying. For the present, however, let us set aside the higher mythic figures of gods and goddesses, and concentrate on the teachers, adepts or masters that are commonly found in meditative and visualising work. These tend, for many men, to be male, just as for many women, the innerworld teachers tend to be female. As always there are no firm rules to such matters, and much depends upon the individual and the techniques employed. One of the most powerful teaching traditions available to a male, for example, involves learning from an innerworld order of sisters or priestesses: this is a quite specific and recognisable branch of the Mysteries, connected to the tradition and Mystery of the Sacred Kingship (Chapter 7).

We should use extreme caution, however, when assessing and when operating with such techniques. Many of the pitfalls and delusions concerning so-called masters are discussed shortly, and the line between beneficial inner work and absurdity, between inspiration and dangerous delusion, is sometimes a very a thin one.

For the present we can set aside specialised contact, such as that of the sisterhood described above, and consider the general technique of contacting and working with innerworld teachers, usually, but not exclusively, appearing as male figures for male students. But what do we mean by 'appearing as male figures'? We dispose of the comic-book nonsense concerning super-males who appear physically to humble grovelling students in order to breed better forms of humanity. At best this level of understanding provides a threshold into the true initiatory techniques and other dimensions, hopefully one which is crossed and then recognised for the delusion that it is. At worst this type of thinking leads to fascism, racism, and what could only be termed evil or black magic. This concept of a male super-human elite plays no part in true spiritual development.

So how do the teachers appear? The answer is through a technique of bridge-building or form-energising. First we must decide what kind of teacher we think we need, and this in itself is no easy task.

Next we should find an image or description of such a teacher: traditionally such images are found in ancient poems, texts, myths and legends, and tend to relate to semi-historical characters. The range of magicians, wise men, warriors, poets, and kings is long. This protean rambling and often vague traditional range is, paradoxically, the safest and most precise to work with. We shall return to it shortly.

Other contacts are those very specific innerworld adepts or teachers that play a role in magical or spiritual orders and groups, often spanning long periods of time. These tend to be more historically defined personae, and there is an advanced technique with which it is possible to tune in to the personae of almost any historical person for innerworld contact, education, and interaction. As this level of working is easily confused, and requires considerable practice, we shall set it aside for the present, merely stating that is not connected in any way to spiritualism. Perhaps the nearest equivalent to this technique is that of ancestral contact found in the primal religions and shamanistic magical arts, or that of the ancestral and hero contacts developed in the classical cultures of Greece and Rome.

Innerworld Teachers

There is a tendency for popular, literary images of innerworld teachers to be very pure, very holy, and very unreal. This is, contrary to what might be believed, a relatively modern and weakening concept. The ancient gods and goddesses, for example, were never stereotypes or idealised images. They did indeed represent certain very specific powers, but always had attached to them or present within them other facets of energy, nature, and even eccentricities of divine personality. Modern psychology has occasionally taken up myth, particularly that of the Greeks, and employed it as a model giving insights into the human psyche and personality. This is fine, but it only goes a very small way towards a true understanding of the gods and goddesses and their potential within human spiritual development.

When we come to innerworld teachers, the picture is more complex. Modern images of pure shining masters are usually part of some money earning or power-grabbing scenario - the old myths, legends and folk tales reveal the true nature of the wise man or woman, and innerworld teachers appear in many guises, just as do the characters in old tales.

A general rule might be as follows. If your innerworld teacher appears as a pure shining superhuman, he or she is almost certainly a fantasy or even a fake. If, however, the innerworld teacher appears to have a comical, eccentric, or over-emphasised personality, through which power is clearly manifesting, then this type of contact is more likely to be genuine. The key is the feeling of true power rather than mere gratuitous eccentricity or frivolity. Certain teachers will often appear in a frivolous even misleading role, but will always offer some deeper sense of identity and purpose to the meditator , which has to be picked up, attuned to, and opened out. After this exchange or period of proving and clarification, the nonsensical aspect of the innerworld contact vanishes, leaving a clearer identity. Teaching may often be given in the form of a game or jest, and may occur during the most superficial or silly first contacts, so we need not assume that all innerworld teaching is solemn or ponderous affair. Indeed, the best teachers always have a deep sense of humour, which is the hallmark of true spiritual development and awareness.

In practice we may encounter innerworld teachers as a result of meditations and visualisations. The contact may be unseen or as far as we are concerned, unconscious; it may be fully conscious, or of varying degrees of mutual awareness in between. Some teaching entities make themselves known to the meditating consciousness only by signs or symbols. These tend to be either non-human beings, or innerworld sources that are working in a far higher octave of consciousness than our own.

In some cases the higher octaves of consciousness will manifest through an innerworld persona, but there is no requirement that this persona be a genuine historical person, even if it presents itself as such.

The simplest and most effective method of working is well established in tradition, and needs only a little adaptation for modern use. Originally, innerworld characters were defined through sets of oral tales, poems, ballads, and ritual drama. These personae were also used in the more advanced stages of imagination, visualisation, and meditation. We all know, for example, of the power of the image of Merlin, a figure from Celtic tradition. He remains powerful even today, despite the accumulated nonsense which overlays the original persona or entity in the popular imagination.[1]

In modern use we can define certain types of persona, types of image. These are built up in visualisation, and eventually take on a life of their own. That is all that there is to it. The imagination attunes to an image, such as those defined in our exercises, and eventually a true inner contact enlivens that image or construct.

When the contact occurs, the image will often change. Some times the true innerworld teacher appears from behind or within, or to one side of the image, and we might dispose of our starting image altogether. Sometimes the image itself intensifies and comes more alive; the entire matter is one for careful judgement and common sense, set into balance with imaginative and intuitive work. Not an easy task, you might say, but we all have an inherent pattern ability or system of imagination and awareness that enables us to perform most of these functions quite naturally.

The degree of energy and ability, however, varies from person to person. It is only if we force our inherent abilities, (in what is assumed to be an act of will-power or some other pseudo-manly notion) that we either get no result, or some type of inflated fantasy. Many typical male inner or spiritual problems arise from the concepts of manliness, will-power, and so forth. Sometimes these enervating notions are disguised in the form of 'purity' or 'transcendent aims'; but they are, nevertheless, still muscle flexing. We need always to remember in this context that the image or Branch of the Warrior is kept in balance by concepts of honour and service. His strength, skill, and discipline is nothing in itself, but everything in service to a spiritual reality greater than the individual. The warrior who ignores this truth becomes a bully, and eventually destroys himself through isolation from the holism of reality.

The Masters

A relatively large proportion of the spiritual and magical literature of our world, ranging from the sources of orthodox religions in both East and West to very recent 'New Age' publications, deals with the subject of the 'masters'.

In formal religion they are defined as saints or demigods; in western esoteric literature the concept of intercession between such beings and higher forms of divinity has tended to be reduced, but the concept of superhuman or transhuman masters has been greatly developed. The entire subject is fraught with problems, and suffers greatly from the power politics of male-dominated orthodoxy. Many men come to the inner arts or traditions of transpersonal development seeking to become masters; few retain or attain this initial desire.

We might first consider if the masters actually exist, and, if they do, what role they play in human life, and what relationship they have to the development of other men along inner transpersonal or spiritual paths. We should first dispose of some of the more pernicious fantasy regarding masters that has appeared in the last 150 years. This is best assessed by briefly examining the difference between earlier concepts of transhuman or highly developed beings, and the relatively modern concepts of innerworld or spiritual or magical masters and adepts.

If we examine the very wide range of literature and tradition available to us on the subject, we find a progressive change occurring, which has greatly accelerated from the nineteenth century onwards, though there are clear indications of it in earlier sources. The most recent concepts of the masters or adepts seem to revolve around superhuman males, usually with an insistence upon physical immortality or immense longevity. These males are said to have special powers, are supposed to oversee the reputed evolution of the human race. They usually live in remote mountainous regions such as the Andes or the Himalayas, but are said to make both physical and non-physical communications to chosen pupils or assistants.

Various cults and movements have sprung up around the central concept a group of masters. The best known of these was the 19th century Theosophical Society, which has had a far reaching effect upon subsequent societies, orders, cults, and upon much of the 'New Age' literature and related practices.

The basic pattern is simple and has been often repeated: someone declares that he or she is in contact with an individual master or group of hidden masters or adepts: the contacted beings communicate teachings and instruction, and encourage the forming of a cult, group, or society. The group develops, disseminates literature and various initiatory techniques, and people use the teachings to develop themselves, or for specific aims within the structure of human society. Usually the boundaries between such intentions are very blurred, and there is a constant shifting of membership as people reassess their own aims and values (at best) or simply become bored with the current fashion that such a group or society represents.

There can be no doubt that unscrupulous money-grubbers can set themselves up to become rich by this simple system; there can also be little doubt that there are many people involved in such groups that genuinely work with sincerity, and truly believe in the structure that they uphold. The reality of the masters, however, is a quite different question to the veracity or honesty of their followers. In some ways it does not matter if the reputed masters are entirely false, for the boundary between a real entity and an imaginative construct is forever shifting; this applies to ourselves as humans just as much as it does to other forms of entity. We shall return to this important concept shortly.

We might tend initially to dispose of the whole subject as immature nonsense, particularly when we consider the range of masters who seem to be readily available to various groups and sects. If we combine these with the large number of saints and demigods and heroes in world religions, we might be justified in asking why these hundreds of superhuman beings have not gained more for the humanity they are supposed to oversee. But let us leave such cynicism aside, and look more deeply at the esoteric or hidden aspects of the subject.

First, there can be little doubt that the prevalence of males as masters or adepts (be they fantasy or fact) is due to the political religious situation of male supremacy. It is significant upon a number of levels that modern mediums or so-called channellers are frequently women, who mediate *male* teachers or masters. We seldom come across a male channel who mediates a female master, or should it be mistress? So ingrained is the concept of male mastership or adepthood, that it often passes unchallenged by otherwise intelligent people who enter into transpersonal or spiritual disciplines. If we are generous, and admit that there may be more to such mediumship than stereotypes of male dominated pseudo-wisdom, then we might see in modern practices the sole remnant of earlier systems of mediumship deriving from the temple and magical practices of the ancient world. In ancient times we know for certain that women often acted as channels for male figures such as gods, heroes, or spirits. We have, however, lost the converse, well established in the past, that men may mediate female energies and entities.

The ingrained concept of the all-male master is a serious block to male development, and until it is totally removed from the individual man's consciousness he cannot make any true or lasting progress upon the inner paths. Once again we touch upon the important subject of balanced polarity: an all male adepthood or sainthood, or an individual male who assumes that he has a right to mastery is essentially a weak unbalanced form. Ultimately a bitter price is paid for such one-sided monosexual development.

In eastern religions there are many female saints or innerworld entities, but they are far less prevalent in the West. In any case these earlier transhuman beings tend to blur with mythic non-human figures. Even historical saints or masters seem to fuse with mythic figures, gods, or in the cases of female saints, goddesses. Somewhere along the line of historical movement, the emphasis has been removed from the mythic and placed upon the fantastic or superhuman.

This change is related to the development of scientific materialism, and though the much popularised masters are supposed to be spiritual entities, they tend to be far removed from the mainstream of human myth and religion, despite their supposed contact with religious traditions of both East and West.

We can detect several strands woven into this changing presentation: the most obvious of these are lust for power, for longevity, for immortality. These desires are projected upon idealised images of super-males. Such desires may, initially, be strong motivations for discipline, learning, and gaining skill, but they are also powerful barriers to true transpersonal realisation.

The situation is a typical initiatory paradox; a man longs for power, longevity, even immortality, but by working through the disciplines that are supposed to lead to such gains, he loses the desire, and it is replaced by a new horizon of consciousness. For a few men this change is, fortunately, gradual. But for the majority of males it comes as a series of drastic initiatory experiences, involving intense catabolic or breaking and destroying forces resonating through not only inner perception, but the entire life pattern, into outer structures such as relationships, family, friends, and work. The very things that he has hoped to gain by becoming a 'master', such as security, freedom, superiority, are all dashed away.

After such painful initiations, we may begin upon the road to true mastery, which is nothing like the popular nonsense found in many bookstores.

4

Polarity and Sexuality

Polarity

Let us consider some of the basics of polarity working within the Male Mysteries. Because we are intentionally working within a male situation,the vital feminine counterparts are defined as innerworld visions, entities, and goddesses. This way of working has both weaknesses and strengths. It must ultimately lead, however, to both sexes working together physically, mentally, emotionally, and spiritually. Many men simply are not ready or able to undertake such work, no matter how willing.

The initiations of the Male Mysteries prepare us and mature us for further spiritual life, by which we must mean all levels of life right through into physical expression, in the broadest human context. Many men damage themselves deeply by seeking to correct problems in their lives through joining groups that offer psychological therapies of various sorts (usually for large sums of money) , group meditation, or visualisation.

Very often men will project and attune themselves and their problems upon female members of the group, when such energy situations should really be adjusted on an inner level first. Traditionally this adjustment is done through work with images, and only at a further stage of development do men and women work together in full or expanding power.

Another frequent problem with men is that they confuse inner forces and simple sexuality. Women seem less prone to obsessive levels of this confusion, though some women do experience it. Many people who simply desire one another like to believe that there is some great magically portentous situation at work, and rather than simply indulge in healthy sexual activity, they concoct increasingly absurd and potentially unhealthy 'magical' or 'spiritual' scenarios and situations for themselves. The favourite one is, of course, 'past lives'. People spend much time agonising over their past lives, and assuming that they are drawn to one another as the result of something in such past lives, rather than the fact there is a simple sexual current between them, even though superficially they may not meet with one another's preconceptions of sexual attraction. Unscrupulous people use past-life scenarios to seduce victims.

In ancient cultures the much misunderstood art of temple sexuality (wrongly called temple prostitution) was used to bring men and women into a full realisation of their own energies, emotions, and spiritual potential. It is rare indeed today for a man to experience this type of initiation from a woman, and probably rarer still for a woman to experience it from a man, but not entirely unknown or impossible. Sexual initiation is a term used freely by anthropologists, psychologists , and social workers, but usually with no concept of its true meaning or potential. What they are referring to, of course, is not actual initiation, but initial sexual experiences which can mould a man's energy pattern for much of his lifetime. Certainly the true sexual initiations should also be the initial sexual experiences of any life cycle, but this seldom occurs.

We might loosely define a typical sequence of development as follows: the male student begins transformation by developing through traditional training and visualising exercises. At a slightly later stage he might work with other men, including but not limited to interaction with and tuition from a more experienced teacher. There is a shocking lack of such group situations for male spiritual and magical development, for we cannot truthfully count those within orthodox religion as being concerned with spiritual empowerment and liberation.

Nothing in the case history of orthodox religion gives us evidence to show that it is remotely interested in human liberty or inner transformation. For such means of development, we have to seek outside formal religion, in the so-called heretical and suppressed cults, in the esoteric and native magical traditions. Clearly this search is fraught with problems and dangers, and of course orthodox propaganda tells us that no man or woman should seek inner development, but that we should remain content to merely worship within a controlled system of soul trading.

However, there is a true case to be made for remaining with a religious orthodox framework. If you have deep belief and your intuition tells you that a particular church or religion will continue to meet your spiritual needs, no one can gainsay this, and you should remain within such a structure. The ways to empowerment and psychic liberation are many, and the esoteric traditions of initiation are not for the faint hearted or weak willed. Indeed, the orthodox propaganda is truer today than ever, for it could be applied to the plethora of money-seeking cults, orders, groups, societies, techniques, channellers, healers, advisers, gurus, teachers, systems, processes and the like that feed off our gullibility, our loneliness, our weakness, our desperate need to find direction in a meaningless and dying world. At least a religion has some ancient spiritual foundation within it, even if it is deeply buried.

Homosexuality

One of the many transforming features within the ferment of the 20th century has been, from the 1960s to the 1990s, an increasing openness and declaration of homosexuality. The feminist pagan movement has frequently associated Goddess worship and the revival of feminine power with lesbian sexual preference. Many gay men associate themselves with the cause of freedom and equality for people of homosexual preference, male or female. We are not directly concerned here with making a social or political study of such declarations and associated movements, but with their inner aspects, particularly where they relate to the Male Mysteries.

There are two issues which seem to have become confused, and which can cause unnecessary suffering and difficulty in terms of inner development. The first issue is that of the simple right of any person, male or female, to express and live his or her sexual preference, providing this does not intentionally harm or damage unwitting or innocent people. The second issue is that of the overall relationship of men and women.

Many feminists, for example, practising Goddess worship deny or reject the possibility of relationships with men, and encourage lesbianism, sometimes suggesting that this is particularly blessed by the Goddess. There is no such open assertion made by modern men concerning worship of the God, but we do find an unhealthy shadowy type of homosexuality running deeply through Christianity and in Christian writings and monastic practices. This is not unhealthy because it is homosexuality, but because it is hidden under the cloak of moralising anti-feminism, and so becomes part of the deep campaign for suppression and denial of the feminine energies in humanity.

It must always be remembered that men suffer from this suppression just as much as women do, though the male damage is often hidden under an illusion of supremacy and false superiority. This illusion of supremacy is reinforced through each generation, but is essentially founded upon fear and imbalance of energies - men have not been allowed to truly touch women, or for that matter, other men, for centuries. No wonder we have such problems in our society. Once the Goddess was removed from recognition in human life, the entire cycle of energies became imbalanced and consequently spun into an unnatural pattern.

One thing we do know; men and women tend to relate sexually to one another; this is simply a matter of polarity, with male and female entities exchanging sexual energies in various ways. The universal Being tends towards polarised, though cyclic and therefore temporary, patterns of energy. In the case of humanity these manifest as body gender, and operate as sexual attraction.

While there is nothing in the Mysteries or in esoteric tradition that condemns male or female homosexuality, there is an immense amount of information on polarity and the use of polarised energies in magical and spiritual development. The techniques of inner development often rely strongly upon sexually polarised imagery. More simply, we are taught that if we use our imaginations powerfully, working with specific sets of images, we will experience transformation. The esoteric traditions uphold special techniques and images which have known results, and which have persisted for thousands of years, though often underground.

While any one of us has a simple right to exercise his or her sexual preference without persecution, no one has the right to suggest that the Goddess especially blesses lesbianism and that men are redundant. Nor is there any right to male political and religious supremacy and a covert homosexuality that suppresses women. We must be constantly made aware of our deep rooted and complex confusions between sexual preference and sexual magic, or between sexual roles in society and sexually defined religious belief. This subject, itself a matter of collective polarities or sexuality, is dealt with in depth in a further book to be published in 1992 by Arcania Press.

In our present context of the Male Mysteries, we need to consider the question of homosexuality as it relates to the techniques which we have suggested for inner development. There is an unfortunate tendency to think that gay men are somehow cut off from magical or spiritual development because of their sexual preference: this is not so. This type of opinion has been voiced publicly by various revivalist pagans, who assume, quite wrongly, that the ancient gods and goddesses are only concerned with heterosexual sexuality as an aspect of fertility and the cycle of nature. The inference is that homosexuality is 'against' the fertility magic of the Old Ones.

This is exactly the type of dangerous nonsense running deeply through orthodox political religion in the West, where homosexuality was loudly condemned yet secretly practised. There are, furthermore, many subtle ramifications to such concepts which appear to be trivial in many ways, yet have a devastatingly powerful effect. When we see such concepts emerging in modern paganism, they are almost undoubtedly the immature hangovers from our materialist Christian upbringing and cultural ambience.

The pagan world seems to have made little difference between homosexuality and heterosexuality; it was all sexuality, and all blessed by the powers of the Mother and Father, no matter by what names the divinities were called . We can see, however, in some aspects of classical Greek culture, the beginning of that Hellenist intellectual trend to male exclusivism, which was eventually taken up by developing Christianity, and warped into the most damaging set of indoctrinations and cruelties that ever passed itself off as a religion of love.

The short answer to this discussion is that each individual is slightly different from any other, and that mature relationships are not based upon stereotypical self-indulgent sex, but upon a wide variety of interwoven factors in which physical sexual activity and gender preference only play a small part.

There is no need for men reviving the Male Mysteries to take a step backwards into the ignorance and prejudice of political Christianity that has dominated the western world for over a thousand years. Indeed, most of the arts and practices of the esoteric traditions derive from pre- or non-Christian sources (without ever denying or rejecting true spiritual Christianity), and if we use them correctly, we can bypass the terrible inheritance of monosexual suppressive religion.

Basic human rights have, in the twentieth century, become confused with deeper realities of polarity and sexuality. This is hardly surprising, as it is only recently that we have been able to talk openly with one another, male or female, and assert sexual rights at all. It is just possible that the men of the twenty-first century may be able to gain a balanced understanding of this problem, for they are emerging from a long period of monosexual religion, deliberately designed to suspend men in a state of vicious immaturity, open to manipulation. Men are, or should soon be, ready to take a huge leap forward.

We might be inclined to think that the use of god and goddess forms, certain male and female archetypes, and the associated techniques described in this book need to be somehow 'reversed' for gay men to use successfully. This is not so, for the archetypes and god-forms both transcend and underpin human sexuality, male and female, hetero- and homosexual. It is often the case that upon inner levels the current sexual preference (be it heterosexual, homosexual, or bisexual) becomes irrelevant. There is always a threshold beyond which our sexual energy becomes aroused in a higher octave with does not require physical gratification. This should not, incidentally, become confused with devious propaganda concerning spirituality and the rejection of the body. In the Mysteries, the body is always sacred, for it is the vehicle of the God and Goddess, who are themselves vehicles of the universal Being.

The open secret for gay men and women in the esoteric tradition is not to try to intellectually alter the images such as god and goddess forms or archetypes and personae, but to use them to gain insight into one's own strengths and weaknesses. The archetypes and divine forms are surprisingly constant through the centuries, and change slowly and organically within the collective consciousness. Furthermore, they are preserved by intentional magical work and concentrated visualisation. This is the difference between a powerful finely tuned archetype and magical image, and the generalised archetypes defined by materialist psychology.

Crude manipulations of the god and goddess or archetypical images, such as those repeatedly made by political Christianity are easily seen as soon as we begin to meditate and emerge from superficial conditioning. A typical example of this manipulation is the removal of the Goddess from worship, other than in her form as Virgin Mother. More subtle examples are found in the imagery of tarot decks, in which certain key pagan images have been corrupted and replaced with suppressive propagandist images.

At a later stage of our inner work in meditation and visualisation, we may, if necessary, reposition images and archetypes upon the Wheel of Life. As a rule the placement of god-forms and archetypes for meditation and visualisation remains inflexible in early training, and only when the individual has a good understanding of, and ability with, the forms and the imaging techniques, do we start moving them around the Sacred Directions, within ourselves, and in dedicated spaces such as a meditation room or temple. For most of us this type of work is done inwardly, and in a very simple sense male and female homosexuality might be said to arise from a variant placing of the archetypes within the energy field. The superficial cause of such variable location of the power images cannot be assessed, it may be represented astrologically in the natal chart, or it may be accessed through deep intuition into past lives, but such methods, and there are many of them, merely give us a rationalisation of inner truths. The key is always to work with the inner truth rather than try to rationalise it or explain it. Most important of all, we must never use systems to try to relate our inner truths to conformists doctrines - that is the way of slavery and destruction.

This aspect of mediation (as distinct from meditation), and magic, in which our inner energies are located as entities and we work with the truth of their relationships upon the Wheel of Life, has not been reassessed for modern use, and holds a vast store of knowledge and understanding which we have yet to unravel.

We must make a firm distinction here between sexual and emotional clarity and maturity, which is potentially within all of us, regardless of our physical sexual preference, and an average male-female sexual polarisation; which can be, however 'normal', replete with viciousness, perversion, cruelty, and delusion. It is the qualities of a person that are important, and how they live and behave with regard to others, not the mere fact of sexual preference.

There is nothing in the Male Mysteries that bars the gay man from development, but there is much within ourselves, heterosexual and homosexual, that may do so.

The ancients made little distinction between sexual encounters of men and women, men and men, women and women. It was all sexuality, part of the flow of energies in nature between different beings. This important concept, however, should not be confused or intentionally warped into a licence for irresponsible sexual behaviour. Too often revival paganism, as a typical example, is little more than a vehicle for the sexual preferences of group leaders and their members. Nothing could be further from the ancient paganism in which sexuality was only a part of a unified view of nature, from the people, to the land, to the planet, to the stars.

There are many possible reasons why Christianity in particular has caused such extreme suppression of homosexuality and bisexuality, while maintaining a distinctly unhealthy corrupting undercurrent of homosexuality for men within the roots of its political and psychological structure. From an esoteric point of view, the rejection of physical love and sexual activity between members of the same sex, especially between males, is perhaps connected to the collection or possession of souls. To elaborate, homosexuality and its suppression goes hand in hand with the concept of the rigid sanctified marriage, female subservience to male dominance, and the demand that women breed without any option of contraception. The general theme seems to be that souls were to be generated and conditioned within one religion only, eventually overtaking all others by sheer weight of numbers.

Historically we find that free sexual expression (but not necessarily selfish indulgence) was often an integral part of the worship of the Great Goddess. Many of the rites and techniques of the ancient temples involved sexuality, though not as in any lurid modern fantasy of such techniques. One of the major aims of developing political Christianity was to remove the souls of humanity from such religion and such rites, the better to control them.

Homosexual males, which is to say physical males with inner polarities that may be predominantly male or female but tend to relate physically to other men, were especially blessed by the Great Goddess. At the risk of generating extreme hostility among modern feminists, including some of my own friends, I would suggest that lesbians might well have been especially blessed by the God - but that this aspect of magical or spiritual polarity has been lost or suppressed.

Part Two

~

The Five Branches

5

WARRIOR, POET, PROPHET, PRIEST, KING

We may summarise the transformative Branches or modes of the Male Mysteries as follows:

1. Warrior 2. Poet 3. Prophet 4. Priest 5. King

These Five Branches focus upon the King as a central or pivotal image, while the Worker or Man is the source and sum of them all. Figure 5 shows the relationships between the Branches. Each Branch has a traditional correspondence to the human body, as shown in Figure 6. These correspondences are of immense value, and show the interplay of male energies.

The Masks and Vehicles

The Five Branches which, for general definition, we have termed Warrior, Poet, Prophet, Priest, and King, are by no means the only harmonics of male entity, but are those which have very specific transformative functions, inner and outer skills, and training techniques for crossing psychic, magical, and spiritual thresholds towards empowerment and enlightenment. Initially we can examine the relationship of the Five Branches to one another, and their collective relationship to the God within, the Bright One.

First we must make a clear distinction between both the specific and relative occupations expressed through or by these Branches, and the inner reality which they embody. More simply we need to be aware that each of the Five Branches does not imply a hard and fast occupation or, in the modern definition, a psychological type, but acts initially as a mirror, and later as a clarifying

Figure 5 - The Five Branches

The Five Branches of the Male Mysteries are: Warrior, Poet, Priest, Prophet, King. The Four Companions of Warrior, Poet, Priest, and Prophet are embodiments of energy in male form, and each has both a goddess and a god within or behind them at deeper levels (see Chapter 10). The King and/or Worker is the primal man, both in his simplest, unrealised state, and in full awareness and balance through the transformations and enabling effects of work with the other branches, companions, gods and goddesses.

The Five Branches are located upon the Tree of Life (see Figure 1), and are broadly associated with the Directions and Elements. These associations are not dogmatic or rigid, and may vary from person to person and time to time, but tend to appear in polarised patterns as shown. They may also be located upon the Tree of Life (see Figures 2 and 5a) which shows the mythic, mental, emotional, and physical harmonic connections.

A further pattern that repays meditation is that of the Horizon or sacred land (planetary surface) and the Underworld and Overworld. The wounded or incomplete King is healed and transformed through the regenerative power of the Underworld, held in balance between Priest above and Prophet below, and the cyclic forces of Poet and Warrior upon the Horizon, to right and left. This holism is shown again in connection to the human body in Figure 6.

*Five is the number of man, by which we should mean not something dominantly male, but male, female and bisexual beings with five digits, able to perform variable manual activities (*Man *and* manual *come from the root word* manus *or hand, with derivatives such as manufacture, manage, manipulate, and manuscript. These are not derived from man as male, but from the Latin word for hand). Unfortunately, the word mankind is seen today as an inclusive 'male' term for humanity, when in fact it means 'handed beings'.*

The four fingers and thumb enable the skills of humanity, through manipulation in the true sense of the word with no negative implications...a musician manipulates his or her instrument, an artist manipulates the brush, a computer programmer the keyboard. Such skills work through polarity or harmonious opposition between thumb and fingers. All mental activity manipulates the stuff of consciousness, thought, emotion, and imagination by our inner equivalent of the hand, the five branches of the will, working through polarity.

The thumb represents the King and Worker, while the four fingers represent the Four Companions.

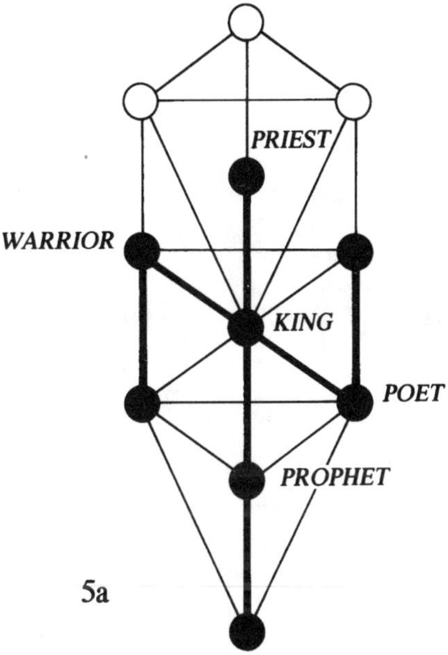
PRIEST
WARRIOR
KING
POET
PROPHET

5a

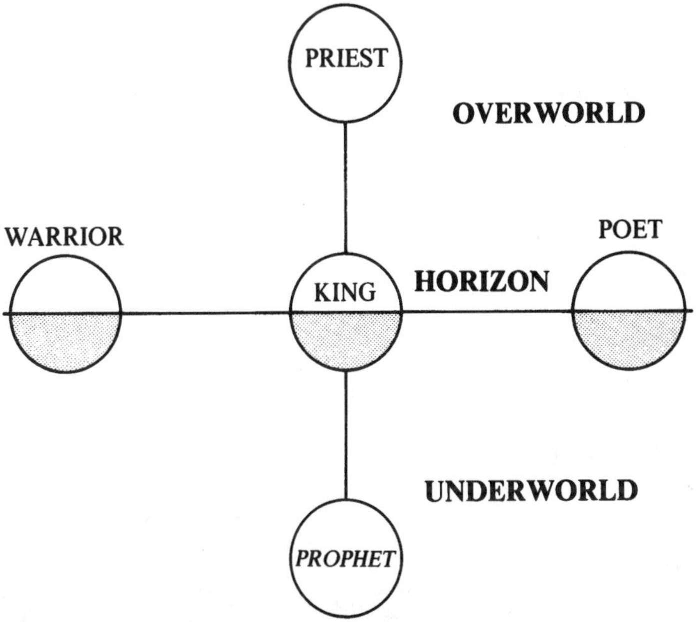
PRIEST
OVERWORLD
WARRIOR
POET
KING
HORIZON
UNDERWORLD
PROPHET

Figure 6 - The Five Branches and the Male Body

Traditional attributes of the Five Branches and the human body are reiterated in modern theories of right and left brain functions. Both the traditional and modern models of man are indications of a deeper pattern of polarised energy within humanity, mirroring patterns of universal being.

1. Head/Priest/Stellar Direction (above)/Spirit or transpersonal being. Third Threshold.

2. Left Hand side (right brain)/Poet/Compassion.

3. Right Hand side (left brain)/Warrior/Severity.

4. Heart/King/Solar Direction (within centre)/soul and mind/Second Threshold.

5. Genitals/Prophet/Lunar Direction (below centre)/sexuality and habitually unconscious mind/Underworld/First Threshold.

6. Feet/Worker or primal man of earth/Sacred Land or planet/outer or manifest form and body.

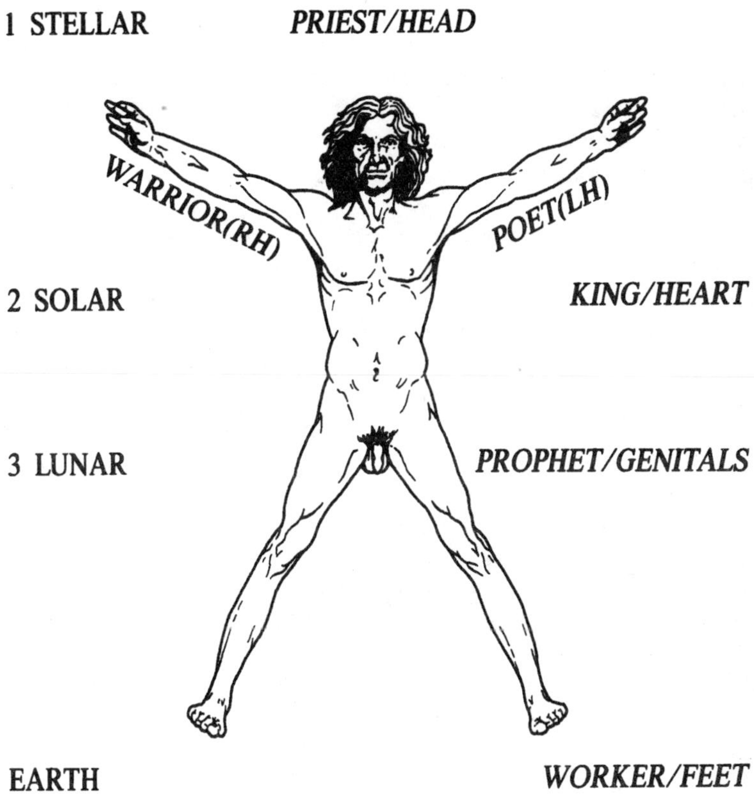
1 STELLAR
PRIEST/HEAD
WARRIOR(RH)
POET(LH)
2 SOLAR
KING/HEART
3 LUNAR
PROPHET/GENITALS
EARTH
WORKER/FEET

lens, for inner forces and their outer expression. Not all poets write or declaim verses, not all warriors defend or kill their fellow men and women, and not all priests mediate true spiritual power. The analogies of mirror and lens are used frequently in magical and spiritual training, and we shall return to them again.

Basically, the images or god-forms that represent the Five Branches are first used in visualisation as ideal figures, as mirrors which we perceive apart from our self-image. At a later stage we turn around, making a complete change of consciousness and direction of attention and energy, and the idealised entity, the image or god-form, becomes transparent within ourselves, now acting as a lens rather than as a mirror. Before this major transition, there are various intermediary stages and techniques of mediation in which we mediate the male images and their energies through ourselves.

This mediation process clarifies our own inner energies and sets them in certain harmonic resonant patterns, thus creating, or more often, unclouding the lens.

This type of working model, which is far more than a mere analogy, can be further developed in terms of the persona or mask, which is at first a cracked or cloudy mirror, even an insurmountable barrier, but later is transformed and rendered transparent to truly mediate that which is within.

Modern society is increasingly fraught with the problems of individuals in occupations that bear little or no relationship to their personalities. This type of separation becomes highly amplified when we move to those levels beyond the personality, and consider the inner Mysteries or spiritual depths of energy and consciousness. Our current culture has very little to offer men, or women, that fulfils or expresses their deepest inner patterns and realities.

In an idealised society, and, as we might assume, in the simple cultures of the ancestral past (which may or may not have truly existed as we envisage them), the inner nature of a man was directly channelled and expressed by his occupation. A warrior took arms because his inner nature was that of the warrior, and so forth. Such primal situations are extremely powerful, for each individual expresses directly his potent inner energies. The persona or mask does not, in such cases, block or deflect the inner nature, but acts as a harmonious filter, lens, or outer presentation for that which is within. To remove such a mask is merely to reveal the higher octave or level of energy that exists within or behind its appearance.

Much of this simple resonance was, in past cultures,

preserved by what are nowadays defined as caste systems, though we need to make a firm distinction between caste as a tool of suppression and slavery, and caste or collective groupings as a spiritual vehicle for skills. Some primal cultures today still have hereditary musicians, poets, warriors, and so forth, though this type of system is rapidly fading from our world. A modern scientist might presume that there is a genetic predisposition among certain families for certain skills. Whereas an esotericist might suggest that the skilled men choose to reincarnate within a certain bloodline and grouping which enables them best to serve their tribe, land, or humanity. Both statements seem, superficially, to imply something similar; two viewpoints of truth that may be defined in different ways according the conceptual and analytic model that we prefer.

The esoteric traditions, however, provide many insights and techniques for awakening awareness and bringing inner change, which are not found in psychology or the materialist sciences. Furthermore, if we limit ourselves to a scientific model, we often cannot access those other levels of awareness, for much of inner development depends crucially upon the imaginative forces. These forces, of themselves, arouse our various levels of energy to thresholds and levels that cannot be obtained through materialist means.

The directly harmonic concept of the personality, as described above, is a far cry from the psychological theory of today; and, of course, our modern personalities are not the simple resonances or holisms that might have been found in an ideal culture or primal past.

The Five Branches and Skills or Crafts

The Five Branches of the Male Mysteries, each of which will be discussed shortly consist of what we might call, in the terminology of an earlier culture, 'noble' categories or classes. There is no suggestion of class snobbism or elitism, and no hint of meritocratic thinking in this terminology. The word noble is used in its proper sense, for the Five Branches purify and ennoble the mind, the emotions, the soul. As in tarot and chess - both ancient magical conceptual structures - the highest and lowest entities or units, the King and Fool, are identical, for both are the page or pawn or primal man ennobled.[6]

When we work in the perennial spiritual or transformative traditions, regardless of which branch of the Mysteries we employ, much of the content is handed down from early cultures and civilisations. Many of the images and concepts in general magical arts, for example, derive from the medieval period and Renaissance, while much of the deeper mythic material derives from Greek, Celtic, Scandinavian, and primal cultures. The higher technology of magic, in the forms of methods and specific systems, derives from Egyptian and, according to persistent widespread tradition, Atlantean civilisations. Thus there are a number of world-views, conceptual models, technical styles and vocabularies, generally preserved (often in a confused state) within the Mysteries or esoteric traditions as we find them today.

In addition to all of the foregoing there is the important but often ignored collective or folk tradition of initiation, which involves ancestral and fairy beings, and the relationship between humanity and the land. This may partake of the more defined streams of tradition, such as those listed, but is often a powerful substratum that works almost independently from specific cultures or civilisations.

The old cultural models, psychologies, mythologies, and cosmologies, require careful assessment and consideration by the modern man and woman. In many cases they act as invaluable correctives to our impoverished, coagulated life conditions and our corrupt, self-destructive culture. But their corrective power must be found upon inner levels, and not outwardly. If we try to live the old cultural or social hieratic or religious systems outwardly, we can easily create situations of almost irresolvable conflict, hostility, and confusion.

There might seem, superficially, to be a rather good case for starting splinter groups or communes living according to the old models of life, but this would be a negative step to take. Just as we are upon a new spiral or turn of human development, so must the patterns represented by the old cultures (embodied within the esoteric traditions) be accessed and activated upon a new spiral, that of the inner imaginative or spiritual dimensions. The old cultures made drastic mistakes, just as we make drastic mistakes, and to materialise them even in miniature is to call up ancient human errors. Upon a higher octave, however, we can merge the best of the old cultures with the seeds of a new pattern for the future. This is the continuity of tradition, not in outer forms and rigid customs, but upon inner levels which flow and remould themselves with each century.

As mentioned above, the Five Branches all work upon and through the normal man, the raw material, the Earth of our Being.

This central and circumference entity is not only what we are, but all that we might be, and all that we ever have been. Thus, a number of initiatory and visualising exercises, particularly those concerned with learning from innerworld teachers, depend upon images of skill and craft, of making and shaping.

In Appendix 2, for example, we find a typical visualisation to put us into contact with a certain type of imaginal or innerworld teacher. These are men of skill or of craft, and not obviously belonging to one of the Noble Branches. But the effect of such teachers is very powerful indeed, and not always in the way that one might expect. Most of these innerworld teachers seem to be concerned with skills or crafts that are no longer used today - the secret lore of animals, the skills of the woodsman, the worker in stone or metal using very simple non-technological tools and methods, the navigator who uses the stars, the gardener, and so forth.

Some teachers, encountered during meditation and guided visualisation, are similar to the ancestors and mentors of humanity represented in primal myth and legend. But we should not rigidly identify them with such mythic beings, or assume that they are 'archetypes' in a modern psychological sense of the word. Some innerworld teachers are certainly of a collective mythic nature, but others seem to be very highly individual and difficult to define by any type of label or generalisation.

In terms of survival we do not seem to need ancient skills today, and no matter how romantic or idealistic we may be, it must be admitted that most of us cannot live in a style even approaching that embodied by these ancestral archetypical or innerworld teachers of skills and crafts. What, therefore, do we learn from them?

While it is possible to learn specific skills and techniques from such innerworld teachers, their main gift to us is one of wisdom, understanding, and insight. This is a subtle subject, difficult to give words to, for much depends upon actual contact and experience. Work with teachers of skill and craft is greatly enhanced by practical work in or approximating to the traditional skill that they represent. For example, there is a very ancient and important rule in magical arts, which is that an initiate should never make his or her living by selling magical services. The actual living is always made with the hands, through a practical skill or craft.

This is not some type of inverted snobbery or dark secrecy and anonymity, but an eminently practical rule. Only through a skill can certain forces manifest properly, and it is essential for the meditator, visualiser, seer, magician, or whatever we care to call ourselves, to have a physical vehicle for his or her abilities. If, as is frequently found today, people ask for money for their inner skills, they are living within a closed circuit situation, and often their abilities fade with the selling.

The Branch of the Priest

The priest is one of most ancient and in many ways least changing Branches of the Male Mysteries, just as priestess is within the Women's Mysteries. We can set aside completely the series of gradually devolving excuses for a changing priesthood that have appeared in decrepit Christianity - priest as social worker, psychologist, moral or political activist, charity worker, counsellor and so forth. These are merely excuses to bolster up a moribund religion clawing to keep its last vestiges of power. In the Third World, particularly Latin America, Christian priests have become militants in a last ditch stand to retain some empire for the Church. None of this, despicable or praiseworthy according to our viewpoint, has any connection to the operation of priesthood, which is a perennial and unchanging ability with well defined disciplines, roles, obligations, and orders or lines of succession.

Priests are usually born with an inherent priestly ability, and it cannot be simply trained into a man in one lifetime. Crossing into the Branch of priesthood is not usually made by sudden leaps in one lifetime as are changes of role in the other major Branches of the Mystery. If we do not have the priestly ability from birth, we may acquire it through gradual inner transformation, to be born with it in a later life. The sudden revelation or blinding vision, often associated with emotional conversions to a standard religion or with entering the formalised orders of an orthodox priesthood, may or may not be a true religious experience. Either way, it does not mean that the person undergoing the experience is suddenly a priest, merely that he has had an unusual vision.

Many men have latent priestly abilities which they choose to ignore, or which are deeply buried by the dross and pollution of our modern way of life. Let us consider how such a priestly nature might manifest itself today.

The priest is essentially someone who, sometimes despite himself, is able to mediate and bring through divine power, the contact of a higher octave of consciousness, or of a god or goddess form or entity. That is all there is to priesthood, an inborn ability to mediate spiritual power. The rest comes with dedication, discipline, and devotion. Like any other talent, we either can or cannot do it. Many lines of priesthood are genetic, descending through family bloodlines over long periods of time. Such genetic lines of priesthood from ancient times tend to mediate very specific god- or goddess-forms, and this can be a very powerful ability and experience indeed once it is properly awakened and,carried out.

The important exception to this old and possibly redundant genetic tendency is the line or order of Sacred Kings, typified in orthodox religion by the little understood figure of Melchizadek in the Old Testament. This line of priesthood cuts across family and racial boundaries, as it is the highest octave of priesthood, merging with and arising from the inner Kingship, the last threshold before encountering the God direct.

Priesthood is associated with the higher centres of energy and consciousness, though it may be innate or an involuntary or unconscious ability in many cases. Thus it is located in the head (see Figure 6), or in some traditional teachings slightly above the physical head of the individual. It is the originating and unifying power for the Right and Left Hand, the poet and warrior. There is a general correspondence of this ancient polarity teaching to modern research into the activities and functions of the right and left hemispheres of the brain.

The Branch or Way of the Poet

The term poet is used here in its oldest sense, quite different from our modern notion of poets, which seems to include all kinds of humorous entertainers who would originally never have been considered poets. The poet is used here to mean the creative individual who makes forms by combining images and expressed patterns. In this category we might therefore include music, for the primal poets were always bardic, using images and music fused together in their art.

The way of the poet is the way of creative discipline, rendering form out of energy, and preserving and communicating that form. It might be as visual art, music, words, or even as dance and movement.

There are many interactions between the Five Branches, and no man is solely of one type or of one Branch. The dancer and the warrior, for example, are very closely related. Both involve great skill, determination, discipline, and above all, highly trained and developed physical co-ordination. The dancer and the warrior share something subtle together too, for both cross thresholds and cause others to cross thresholds through their body movements.

In ancient times the poet was a combination of musician and creator of verses (originally, written poetry did not exist). There is a typical modern delusion that such ancient poets were crude folksy rhymsters, and many modern men go through a simplistic phase of poetry in which they try to ape this utterly spurious simplicity, a type of poetry that never existed in the first place, and is solely the product of modern sentiment.

In fact the primal poet and musician was a man to be feared and respected. The power of making and unmaking was in his breast and upon his tongue. So few modern poets come anywhere near this terrifying threshold, that we might be excused for wondering if the power of poetry has almost abandoned our world.

In the individual the power of the poet is traditionally that of the left hand - the artistic and imaginative qualities of a man (see Figure 5 and 6). The left hand is the area or energy of the feminine forces of the male psyche. In mystical or divine attributes upon the Tree of Life (Figure 2) , the left hand pillar is feminine, flowing from the Great Goddess, while the right hand is masculine, uttered by the God. This polarity pattern was recognised and used in meditation and spiritual training many centuries before modern theories of animus, anima, or right and left brain potentials were formulated.

The Branch of the Prophet

While the Poet is both the memory and inspirer of his people, the Prophet is the conscience. It is often assumed, quite wrongly, that prophets are solely concerned with foretelling the future; this is only one aspect of prophetic consciousness.

It seems that prophets, in a strict definition of the term, are almost without exception male. We must exercise extreme caution with such conclusions however, as history has been heavily doctored and twisted by orthodox male dominated religion for the last thousand years or more. The sybils, or female prophets, of the ancient world seem to have worked in a different way from their male counterparts. A difference which we will examine shortly, and which may be due to those polarities of physical gender which make specific changes and definitions of inner energies whenever such energies manifest. The energies may be identical but they will tend to manifest in different forms according to the gender of the human prophet or sybil.

None of the foregoing implies any stereotypical roles or inflexible sets of laws. Furthermore, the boundaries, thresholds and exchanges between male and female are fluid, changing through the ages both collectively and individually. Such changes tend to be very slow and long-term, and we are in a particularly difficult position to judge them at present due to the confusion resulting from a long period of imbalance which has harmed men and women through an over-emphasis on totally false 'masculine' qualities.

One thing is certain, there are clear indications of a change of collective and individual awareness at present. It seems to be reaching towards a higher octave or spiral of a period which slowly came to an end about three thousand years ago, when most human societies were still, broadly speaking, matriarchal, as shown by the fact that the Great Goddess was the ultimate aspect of divinity then identified by humanity. The last fifteen hundred years of militant, dogmatic, political, Christianity in the West, is the final manifestation of forces that tended to destroy the older Goddess orientated cultures and replace them with those in which men claimed a spurious innate superiority. This final manifestation includes materialism and materialist sciences, which are the direct products of Christian and monotheistic religion, rather than the opposites or antagonists that they are often labelled as.

The male prophet often sees that which is ignored by most other men, feels the impending disasters that may be averted, and makes painful but direct contact with other states of Being, particularly those which humanity calls either Underworld or Divine.

He does not do this solely through intuition, but through a different rate or faculty of consciousness which may manifest through intuition, intellect, emotion, or through what are nowadays obscure techniques and symbolic structures of communication. If we consider the ancient world briefly, we find that sybils tended towards divine possession or mantric trances, in which the presence of a god or goddess fills the priestess (sybil) and takes over her regular persona, suppressing it entirely. This is similar in some ways to modern mediumship or channelling, but it must be stressed that the presence of a god or goddess in a human body is rather a different degree of power to the dreary presence of most 'spirit guides'.

In the Celtic and classical cultures, as in some primal rites today, the presence of the god in a human form was a terrifying experience, not to be taken lightly, and was always clearly understood to be quite different from the communication of spirits, ancestors, heroes, and other lesser entities.

The male prophet, however, tends not to be a physical vehicle for a god or goddess form, but to make some kind of connection to the deity or power concerned without displacement or total suppression of individuality. The names, types, or definitions of deity are irrelevant in such circumstances, for the vision of God or Goddess is, thankfully perhaps, always filtered through a cultural environment and racial set of symbols and beliefs. Though there is a vast amount of active propaganda concerning orthodox, politically enforced gods and their much-vaunted universality, they are still clearly racial and local in their history, origin, and behaviour.

A small number of mystics and visionaries, however, can gain access to the true universal consciousness and Being by reaching through and beyond these flawed local daemones that pass themselves off as universal omnipotent gods or Gods. It is well worth noting in this context that very few of the ancient gods claim universality or omnipotence. This simplicity is usually thought to be due to their assumedly primitive, limited nature, and to the lack of development of those people who worshipped them. Yet specific god-forms are extremely powerful and can be of enormous benefit to the development of human beings, without ever claiming universality. This situation is central to the male mysteries and will repay much meditation. Male imbalance as we know it today,and as it manifests in myriad forms throughout our western world, was considerably accelerated as the result of a simple tribal god being declared universal. This is a very subtle tool of suppression indeed, for all the many images and energies which were inherently transformative and liberating were suddenly 'lesser', or even 'evil', and so could be banned, perverted, expunged, ignored.

The prophet is one of those few chosen men who are not a superior or elite brotherhood, but considered by many (including themselves sometimes) as accursed and mad. In a man, the prophetic consciousness is uncontrollable and comes and goes as it will. He is often driven temporarily mad by such visions and by the opening of his perception to human pain and suffering.

Regrettably, the way of the prophet is one of those by which dangerous delusions of glamour and grandeur can overtake a man's ego and ultimately destroy him. Many weak men choose to pretend to be prophets. They do not need the skill and discipline of the warrior, or the training and artistic talent of the poet, to support their claim. Prophecy, like New Age channelling and spiritual mastery or so-called immortality, has long been replete with frauds, charlatans and deluded simpletons. The true prophet is known by one particular hallmark - he is almost always unwilling to receive his prophetic gifts and transcendent or transtemporal understanding. A very small number of prophets come to terms with their talent, and may mature through it and be able to cope with it. In many men, the prophetic energies wane after a certain age - the onset is usually puberty and the waning period is often in the mid-thirties. Prophecy is closely linked to sexuality and polarity.

We need not presume that the prophet is totally filled with cosmic insights; he is the young man who sees the evil of war and makes his protest felt, wondering why all those around him cannot see and are opposed to his opposition. He is the campaigner for the environment, the man who withdraws from the social and economic struggle, not because he fails, but because he sees beyond the spurious values and the complex strands of enslavement that such a struggle involves. More rarely nowadays, he is the visionary man of politics, but this type of prophet should be regarded with extreme caution, and it is one of the most likely areas to be filled with ego, fraud, deceit, and delusion.

Traditionally we find that prophets were often warriors or poets, and there is a direct transition from warrior or poet to prophet within every man. It comes through terrible pain and hardship, and is catalysed by compassion for the suffering of others.

In the individual man, prophecy is associated with the genitals, the Lunar centre, and the mysterious Underworld. When a prophet is inflamed with inspiration, the sexual energies rise up to the solar or king centre (see Figure 6). Under specific circumstances and with training, the energies will rise into the head centre. The reflex or polarity between Prophet and Priest is that the Underworld energies are spontaneously uttered through the mouth of the Prophet. In simpler terms we have all experienced this, for it occurs as the sudden truth that we blurt out willy- nilly.

The Warrior

The Warrior is the most popular, visible, obvious, yet most frequently confused Branch of the Male Mysteries. Much of this confusion in popular imagination arises from a single-sided development of the warrior image, usually with false emphasis placed upon physical attributes and skill at violence.

More space has been given to the Branch of Warrior simply because this seems to be the most prevalent branch in modern man, either in fact, or in terms of valid or invalid aspirations. The Warrior is traditionally associated with the right hand (see Figures 5 and 6) powers of strength, reason, physical development and so forth. He needs to be balanced by the left hand of the poet. At later stages of development he may consciously relate to the central or spinal branches of King, Prophet, and Priest.

In an ideal or idealised society, where people seem to have well defined interacting roles, the warrior group, caste or class is often held in balance by other groups and their functions. The individual warrior finds harmony for his outgoing and dynamic energies through such interactions and relationships, which are often non-personal and non-sexual. One of the problems in modern practice is that as soon as we use words like 'relationship' there is a tendency towards a sexual connotation. This is the result of centuries of sexual repression and imbalance, as a result of which we place a vast over-emphasis upon the role of physical gratification and emotional attachment, both of which are the most superficial levels of relationship and sexuality.

At this superficial or outermost level, the suppressive and enervating stereotypes of sexuality and sexual roles come into play, and we need to destroy such stereotypes for ever. This task is, in itself, one for strong and persistent skilled warriors to undertake. In the earliest ideal societies or cultures, of course, warriors were not exclusively male, and we shall examine some specific models, returning to them in various contexts.

Such idealised societies, held together by transpersonal concepts and spiritual values, do not, of course exist today, if indeed they ever existed. Nevertheless, we can look to models of idealised societies or images from history to give us insight and inspiration concerning the roles of the Five Branches. On an inner level the personal balance of a warrior is gained through a combination of action and stillness, and such techniques are still widely taught in the martial arts of the East today. Far less well known, however, and less publicised, are the powerful techniques once practised in western culture for the spiritual warrior. Regrettably, politics and religion have shrouded this important Branch of the Male Mysteries in ignorance and in vicious delusion.

Perhaps the best known western examples presenting such techniques, albeit in a rather rarefied literary form, are the early texts concerning the court of King Arthur, the orders of knighthood, and the Quest for the Holy Grail. These often mask a pre-Christian tradition of the spiritual warrior[7], rooted in Celtic and early European history and myth. To a lesser extent we also find such techniques in the classical myths of the Greek and Roman worlds, though these have suffered much through repeated editing and misinterpretation over the centuries.

The Warrior and the Ideal or Model Society

The idealised society, aspired to, dreamed of, or, more rarely, deliberately used in visualisation, also acts in many ways as a model for individual and social or group maturity. It works in a very direct and simple way, through personal or collective development of those qualities represented by the personae or roles found within that model society. One of the best known models of this sort was that of the perfect spiritual city in which the Grail is found. We shall return to this model again. Philosophers have sought to intellectually define such perfect cultures or social entities, as in Plato's *Republic* [8], while at the other extreme of consciousness, mystics and visionaries perceive such perfected places instantly in fits of inspiration, joy, and terror. As with all such images, there can be an inversion or perversion - the shadow image. The concept of the elitist heaven or heavenly city into which the elect are gathered, is one obvious example of such corruption and manipulation of a mythic image towards suppressive ends.

The technique of visualising and working towards the idealised culture or society was widely used in mystical and magical training, and in many cases the imagery attuned to real entities, real cultures, actual worlds and dimensions. Nowadays, we tend to take a more psychological approach to this type of developing model, and so lose much of the power inherent in the ancient methods, which were never confined to a purely mental or emotional level, but had the potential to bridge between the human awareness and that of other entities in other states of existence. Even if we set this important aspect of the perennial traditions aside, there is still great empowerment in these idealised images of people within idealised social and physical structures.

One subtle operative function is that of the physical structure, its proportions, its allocation of the Four Directions and so forth. Spiritual or magical cities, lands, zones, and structures, are seldom random. Originally, people intentionally but naturally reflected this holistic pattern-making - which attuned both human and geomantic forces - in the actual structure of their cities and the harmonic areas or divisions of the land. Thus in ancient Ireland or ancient Greece, we find that certain zones, directions, or tribes, are specifically those of the warriors, musicians, poets, magicians, and so forth.

The allocation of the Directions is discussed in Chapter 6 and shown in Figure 1.

The Role of the Warrior

In western culture we find the role of the warrior and hero highly emphasised in history from the most ancient times. In modern history, the soldier or hero takes on a very political role, and in most recent times is regarded, at worst, as a creature of futility and degradation, the professional killer and suppressor of the weak, and at best as an innocent victim of unscrupulous manipulators, who send young men to die in vast numbers for false causes, with secret purposes of aggrandising profit and personal power being crudely masked by patriotism, religion, and political jargon.

But at one time the role of warrior and hero (hero being a very concise term to which we shall turn later) merged with that of the sacred king. The warrior who dies in certain circumstances may become absorbed into the Branch of the Sacrificial Kingship. In such circumstances his death frees him from the imbalances of his life, and purifies his spirit, through his dedication to the benefit of the people for whom he dies. This is, nowadays, an obscure and often misunderstood concept, one which may be easily abused by propagandists and unscrupulous manipulators: it reappears in many contexts in the Male Mysteries.

The Warrior is the Branch suited to the physically active, fit and generally outgoing individual. But this is merely the initial stage of the path, often entered into during youth. It seems a terrible fate that our modern men of great physical skill, such as sportsmen, only have a short working life. They become highly over-developed for a few years, in the hope of earning vast sums of money: but after the first phase of their life (from Youth into Adulthood, see Figure 1) they are already discarded, outlived, burnt up. This elite level of the problem is reflected generally in many young men who go through a phase of physical skills, only to lose such interest and fitness in their late twenties or thirties, and to become sluggish and immovable once the obvious vigour of youthful sport has, apparently, left them.

The true development of the Warrior, however, is clearly indicated in the wisdom traditions of both East and West. The physical skills and martial abilities, developed through long training, are all aimed at a transformation of consciousness. The reason why our modern sportsmen and highly physically skilled men, or indeed the youthful sportsman who becomes a sluggish adult, all fail to develop beyond a certain age, is nothing to do with physical degeneration or ageing itself. The problem is that the attitude and training is all directed outwardly - skill to gain praise, skill to earn money. The warrior training of earlier cultures was certainly aimed at building skills, and to develop young men into skilled fighters and defenders, but it had many deeper levels which persisted and developed through the entire lifetime. A true warrior never retires, but moves the development of skill and understanding inwards, until he achieves harmony by unifying the warring aspects of his self: this then becomes the state of inner kingship through which the Bright One, the inner divinity, may at last appear.

In the Grail legends we find this traditional training and aspiration stated in a curious fusion of pagan and Christian lore. The knight, the warrior, with his vigour and skill at arms, must give up seeking military glory, and quest after the unattainable. The Grail, seen at first as a physical vessel or treasure, is found to be a spiritual condition; yet it is associated with the idealised city, the geomantic power place, and has a true physical and metaphysical existence in its own right. In other words, it is not what we moderns would call 'a state of mind' or what the orthodox religious might have called 'a state of grace'. These merely help the aspirant to perceive or make brief contact with the Grail.

The preparation for this inner realisation is not only in the physical skills, but in the ethical and spiritual rules absorbed by the warrior. Let us examine these briefly, for they are central to the Male Mysteries in any form, at any time, in any place or world.

The warrior is under many strict rules, all ultimately leading to a sense of true responsibility. He and he alone is responsible for the outcome of his actions. The physical skills are dependent upon long hours of practice, until the coordination, the harmony of body and mind, lead to a fusion of vital energies and consciousness, giving a transpersonal or spiritual experience, an initiation of higher consciousness. This comes through perfect motion, impersonal skill, a state of pure being which may be attained through physical development combined with meditation. Many other skills involving movement relate to this.

The strength and skill of the warrior are kept from overspilling into random action through a set of simple but potent rules: he must defend the weak; he must use his power and skill only to beneficial ends; he must be able not merely to control his emotions, but to transmute them, to be aware and alert in inner states beyond emotion. In early training these qualities are reinforced by vows, by rules, by the presence and advice and, if necessary, admonition, of senior mature men. In the case of the ancient Irish warriors, the training was carried out by warrior women, a subject which is described in detail in the legend of Cuchulainn, an invaluable source of material for the Male Mysteries.[7]

But through meditation and proper training, the ethical and spiritual values become more than mere conditioning, for the warrior gains insights into truth, into relative conditions of reality. He understands that the stronger and more powerful an individual or group becomes, the more such power must be guided by compassion, by non-selfish ends.

This deep realisation and teaching is found in western tradition in the courtly and knighthood rules, well known in medieval and later literature. The fact that such rules were greatly abused and ignored, even while giving lip service to them, does not alter the validity of the code itself. Just as there are weak and cowardly bullies and monsters in every age, so are their always a number of true warriors, perfect knights. Ultimately the warrior must be willing to die to protect the people: this is the same ethic of compassion and non-personality that is at the heart of non-violent ways such as Buddhism. It is interesting to realise in this context, that many warrior skills are found in a non-violent context. The same concepts are hidden deep within the knightly code of the west, which derives from the warrior code of the ancient Celts and Greeks.

If we delve far back into the world of our ancestors, we find a very different attitude to life and death to our own. In the Christian era the warrior or knight was often encouraged to meditate upon death, a meditation firmly linked to orthodox religion.

This political conditioning often led to terrible results; the murder of non-believers and the military persecution of other races. The knightly code, however, aimed to transcend physical death, to show how irrelevant it is. And little wonder, for the knightly code is founded directly upon the heroic warrior code of an earlier world, exemplified by the Celtic and Greek heroes. These warrior codes were firmly rooted in a matriarchal goddess-worshipping culture; we frequently find that the warrior training and spiritual inspiration was under the control of women, both as human, superhuman and divine beings.

The most terrifying goddesses of the ancient world were often warrior goddesses, and we need to be very cautious when we encounter modern divisive scenarios which say that patriarchal militaristic men destroyed the old goddess culture. The evidence of warrior goddesses, fusing the powers of life, sexuality and death, inspiring and training heroes, warriors, and prophets and poets, is clear from early cultures. Thus no one who has truly examined what we know of such cultures can claim that they became divisive, with aggressive men eventually destroying the non-aggressive goddess civilisation either from within or from without.

Essentially the concept of aggression is likely to be a modern retrospective attribute. The great goddesses of sexuality and death, such as the Irish Morrigan, the mythic warrior women who trained young men, such as the Scottish Schathach, and the classical goddesses of war and cultural development, wisdom and knowledge, such as Minerva or Athena, were not divinities of 'aggression'. Indeed the developing image of this group of goddess, very central to the Male Mysteries, reaches from a savage but impersonal goddess of the life and death within the sacred land, to a calm and wise goddess (Athena). She masked the primal, powerful warrior skills and forces, mediating them as she wished, including the direct protection, education and initiation of chosen men.

For modern use we may, with some caution but also with powerful results, turn to the earlier code of warrior conduct embedded within the classical and Celtic myths that tell of such goddesses and their chosen male trainees, initiates, or heroes. There are a number of reasons why the world-view of a very early culture may be valid today. On the more obvious levels we find that it bypasses the corrupt areas of political religion, often acting as shock treatment to jolt us out of our materialist complacency, a complacency sitting uncomfortably on the surface of deep unrest and confusion. Second, the passage of cultural or collective growth is not a straight line but a complex of inter-linked spirals. More simply, we are at a turning point similar to that of two thousand years ago, the threshold between the pagan and Christian eras in the West. It is possible to tap into the energies and primal concepts of our ancestors through the law of octaves: we are now where they were, but at a different harmonic or octave level.

The primal attitude to life, death, battle, and warrior skills, is central to the development of modern men: otherwise we are returning to deadening and vicious traps that we found when we entered this world.

To the Warrior as Hero

Heroes play a large part in the mythology and legendary history of our world. In recent years it has become fashionable to laugh at the hero, and in modern film and fiction to delight in the 'anti-hero'; this is because we have seen through the false hero, but have not yet recovered the true hero.

The false hero is the sexual all-male stereotype with bulging muscles, jutting jaw, all decision, action, and little or no emotion or introspection. These types appear frequently in early films: gentlemen detectives, war heroes and so forth. They also dominate much of early twentieth century popular fiction. We may rapidly set such images aside...they are a dead end.

Primal heroes, however, are a different matter. They embody certain strengths and weaknesses that are inherent in every male. Many of their legends reveal much to us concerning initiation, spiritual growth, emotional maturity, and humankind's relationship to both environmental and apparently supernatural forces. Many heroes are the sons of divine beings, often of a union between one human parent and one divine. Such unions reveal a great deal of information on ancient methods of initiation and transformation...they are not mere allegories or superstitions.

In modern terms, we may look at the inherent character of the hero through the ages; certain persistent fundamental qualities and actions define a hero...even down to our modern stereotypes who pale into insignificance beside their ancestral counterparts.

What Makes a Hero?

A hero is, usually, a warrior of some sort, usually but not inevitably, a trained fighter, bearer of arms. There are, of course, heroes who never lift a weapon or fight a physical battle. Their heroic deeds are, nevertheless, still definable and recognisable. The hero has certain strengths, be they of muscle or will, brain or body. But he is also unfailingly motivated by gentleness and compassion, without which he is merely an unfeeling thug or a soldier pawn in the hands of unscrupulous manipulators. He protects the weak, assists them, and will, if necessary, sacrifice his own interests, even his life, to protect defend and benefit others.

These qualities are ell essentially nurturing, they are those of the mother...feminine qualities. The hero is not a superman, he is a highly empowered active dynamic male whose maleness is balanced by feminine qualities, feelings, and abilities.

In some legends we find this truth exemplified by the relationship between a hero and a goddess. The Irish hero Cuchulainn, for example, has astonishing powers, skills, strength, energy, sexual prowess, beauty, and so forth. But he fails to recognise that a major part of his potential is realised through the blessing and protection of the Morrigan, the primal goddess of sexuality and death. Because he fails to recognise her, both literally during several meetings, and of course inwardly, she eventually withdraws her blessing and protection. Through his failure to identify the goddess, Cuchulainn loses much of his supernatural strength and skill, and so may be killed by his enemies.[7]

This theme recurs frequently in the Arthurian and Grail legends of later medieval literature: the feminine qualities, the mysterious powers of the goddess, are essential for the king, the knight, the hero. Without them he is incomplete, a one-sided stereotype. The sword Excalibur is nothing without the Scabbard: Arthur is weakened and destroyed without Guinevere, and so forth.[9]

We might take this today as a reminder that the right hand (the swordhand of the Warrior) is imbalanced without the left hand (the scabbard-hand of the feminine, shown as the Branch of the Poet).

6

THE WORKER AND THE WHEEL OF LIFE

The Worker - His Skills and Crafts

The Five Branches pattern used in this book is not, of course, the only possible model that might define masculine entities, roles, and related energies or states of consciousness. Environmentally defined and balanced systems were well known in early cultures, depending upon caste (in a non-elitist sense to which we shall return shortly), occupation, and, interestingly, geographical or spatial location. Early societies orientated their settlements, cities, territories and lands according to sacred directions and geomantic locations; specific castes or occupations were often located in specific Quarters or Directions.

A typical example would be that of ancestral Ireland, with the royal court in the centre of the land, and the various castes or occupations laid out according to the Sacred Directions of East, South, West, and North. This spatial pattern has its inner or metaphysical geometry, for the Directions corresponded to the four Elements of Air, Fire, Water, and Earth, and to the four seasons of Spring, Summer, Autumn, and Winter. This four-fold Elemental pattern is found in a developed expression in the Tarot, where the personae or Court Cards correspond to certain relative human types, interacting in an Elemental relationship to one another (see Figure 1). On a deeper level, the human Elemental personae become archetypes or primal god and goddess forms. Tarot is merely one example of a highly developed psychology pre-dating materialist models of the psyche such as we have today. By a typical inversion of standards, modern psychology seeks to 'explain' these earlier models, as if they are not effective or comprehensive in their own right.

Our four major Branches of Warrior, Poet, Prophet, and Priest, are male archetypes or innerworld forms for specific energies. They actually stand at the Cross-Quarters of the Circle: we might begin with the Warrior in the South East, the Poet in the South West, the Prophet in the North West, and the Priest in the North East. In the centre is the King.

The positions suggested are not rigid or dogmatic, and in visualisation and special ceremonial or ritual pattern making work, we may find that they change position. The overall pattern described, as shown in Figure 6, is the basic set of relationships of the Five Branches or Beings. The seasonal attributes are very important in this context, and the relationships and harmonies or polarities should always be linked to the concept of Sacred Space and the Wheel of Life, as in Figure 1. Lists of correspondences are fruitless without an overview or unifying model, such as that of Sacred Space and the Wheel of Life.

The seasons combine the phases of energy in the land (due to planetary rotation relative to the Sun) with the phases of birth, adulthood, maturity, and old age in a human being. When we work with such holistic models, they slowly transform all levels of our perception, and generate a deep sense of connection and rhythm between every aspect of life within and around us.

The seemingly missing person in our structure of relative male archetypes is of course, the basic man, the Worker. Originally he would have been the peasant, labourer, farmer, huntsman, or craftsman. The worker group also has,within itself, a fourfold or multifold spiral of directions and relationships. Holistic structures and patterns mirror the whole within each part.

In the Mysteries, the worker, the labourer, the basic man, is of course ourselves. Thus he is the simplest level of male entity, but also the most complex and all inclusive. The King and the peasant are one and the same person, the work is whatever we do within ourselves, moving towards transformation. Thus we are worker and work, material, and craftsman.

Losing Power

Let us look at one of the most typical problems that men in general have today; loss of power and identity. What is there in the broad range of the Male Mysteries that can resolve situations, both inner and outer, that bring loss of power?

The most significant areas in which the traditional male initiations and practices can work are the inner levels of being. Most males are totally dependent upon exterior circumstances for their sense of identity; when these circumstance are changed or disempowered, the man collapses. This situation is found in men of all abilities, social groups, and levels of power and intelligence. It applies as strongly and as terribly to the labouring man who loses his job as it does to the executive who is defeated in a boardroom struggle.

We find this sorry situation reflected in a much broader way in the emblems of the consumer society, in which we are all, male and female, encouraged to assess our worth by the objects which we own, by the image which we assemble through these objects, ranging from work, to home, to clothes, and body image. Reassurance is found, we are repeatedly told, by looking at the objects that we own, at the status that we have, at our face and body in the mirror, and seeing that they are good. The levels of indoctrinated value are subtly in flux, for they are moulded by the profit motive of the entities, such as, but not solely limited to, commercial ventures that sell us such images.

The outer shell has, somehow, become the main focus of entity for men, and when it is broken, they often die. It is a simple truth that many men, upon retiring from dull, deadening, trivial, and utterly pointless work, in which they have remained for a major part of their life simply to scrape a living, lie down and die. Their reason for living, sordid and trivial as it was, has been taken away from them. Social and psychological studies of this phenomenon have been made, but it is really the most obvious expression of something that happens in every man repeatedly whenever he loses power or an exteriorised reason for his existence.

Whenever a man loses power, loses an exterior focus, he dies. In the final case, he dies physically, but during his lifetime a man will die and be reborn a number of times.

This is a powerful feature of human energy and/or consciousness, male and female, but it manifests more distinctly in males. Women have a continuity and rhythm that men, at present, lack. A man tends to mature by fits and starts, while a woman tends to mature in a steady progression. Thus, if we take a theoretical man and theoretical woman, they might begin a life cycle at the same level of awareness. The woman is more likely to make rhythmic steady progress towards maturity and understanding: sometimes the man will be far behind the woman, at other theoretical points in time, he will have leapt ahead.

This pattern is found again, in higher and lower octaves, upon the inner levels, with spiritual cycles of development, death and rebirth. Men can make long leaps into the unknown, but women are able to move through a continuum, a holism, a pleroma.

Furthermore, for the male, it is literally the unknown into which he leaps, but the female is able, to a certain extent, to sense what lies beyond such thresholds. This obscure sexual relationship was epitomised in the ancient sacrificial rites, in which a priestess officiated over the sending of the male spirit into the otherworld. Some of this subject is covered in our chapter on the Sacred Kingship (page 79).

On a physical sexual level we find this manifesting through the male orgasm, which tends to be a single explosive event, while the woman is capable of repeated orgasm. The magical link between sexuality and death has been observed but totally misunderstand in materialist psychology, probably reflecting the lusts of the observers rather than any truth concerning human psychic energies and patterns.

On a metaphysical level, we find that gender or polarity is a matter of *shape*, just as it is upon the outermost physical manifestation, though there are many harmonics or levels in between. Metaphysics, and the perennial models used in metaphysics, magic, and mystical cosmology, and their related contemplative exercises, all affirm and rely upon certain primal universal patterns: the point, the line, and the circle. We still call this geometry today, after the ancient Greek manner, but such sacred geometry has a universal expression and truth. Geometry means the measuring of the earth, but the earth or world concerned is not limited to the surface of our planet, it is the universal World, of which our two dimensional geometry is merely a working analogy.

This inherent power within properties of shape is found again in the implements of magical ceremony, usually the sword, rod, cup, and shield, and the mobile shape of the cord. These are, in a pure shape sense, the line, the circle, and the surface. Such properties of shape and movement manifest in us as energies, as consciousness, and of course, as gender. The male shape is, outwardly, that of the rod or line, shown sexually by the penis. The female shape is, outwardly, that of the cup circle or spiral, shown sexually by the vagina. There is no suggestion here that these are limiting or all-inclusive stereotypes, merely that such universal shapes are relatively manifested through gender.

There is no question that men and women have both male and female shapes and energies within them, in the endless relative patterns and ramifications of humanity, and on to broader patterns within the holism of the land, the planet, the solar system, the universe.

But the rod or line is only relative, the cup or vagina is only a relative shape within a fullness of other shapes, all mutually defining one another in a changing resonant flow. That linear leap made by a male when he dies and is reborn to a new level of realisation, is in truth a spiral. That universal spiral of the Great Mother is, in truth, an infinitely long line, spiralling into a circular matrix. These seemingly abstract truths are properties of energy, and are revealed today as relative laws or tendencies by our most advanced physics. Thus the scientific materialist levels of research have at last come a full circle, to confirm that which was always taught in the Mysteries. Now that science is destroying its very foundations of pseudo-masculine logic, men can begin to die and be reborn onto a new level of understanding.

The Wheel of Life and the Seven Directions

The Wheel of Life relates the Four Elements, the seasons, the Directions, and various states of power. It also relates through its ceaseless turning, the phases of a life cycle, both for gods and humans. Traditionally, certain images are located in certain Quarters of the Circle or Wheel. In western magic this concept is fundamental; and in magical and spiritual training worldwide, the concept of the Seven Directions occurs repeatedly. The Wheel, as we see in Figure 1, appears to have only Four Quarters, those of the East, South, West, and North. But it is a flat glyph or map completed by the presence of a human standing within it at the centre. It is, in fact, a definition of our standing position and zone of awareness; thus it represents the surface of the land or planet, and the sphere of awareness or being. This sphere ultimately embraces the universe, though most of us are content to settle for a sphere of awareness that is a little smaller.

The Seven Directions, then, are Above/Below, East/West, South/North, and Within. God-forms and images are related to each Direction. More traditionally we would say that the gods are found in these directions - that they dwell there naturally.

The Circle or Wheel and the Tree of Life are part of one another - the Tree grows in the centre of the sphere - it is both the upright human with the stars above and the land below, and the Axis Mundi, or pivot of the worlds, through the centre of the Solar System. (For Gods upon the Tree of Life, see Chapter 9.)

East

In the East we find gods of Spring, change, turbulence, swiftly moving force. The Element is Air, which is both Breath of Spirit, and the howling hurricane of destruction. The gods of Air are frequently associated with warrior skills, and therefore have a further level of honour, protection of the weak, defence of the victim against the oppressor. Because Air is also the Element of communication, in terms of speech, music, and more subtly, consciousness or swiftly moving thoughts, we find messenger gods and teacher gods, and communicator gods in the eastern Quarter. The techniques and forces of arousal, be it sexual or intellectual, are taught and enabled by the gods of the eastern Quarter.The magical implement is the Sword or Arrow.

South

In the South we find gods of ascension, of Summer, of light, of balanced power. The Element is Fire, both in the form of the burning flame, the midsummer sun, and the universal power of Light. The gods of this Quarter maintain a balance and harmony of the fiery powers, and are concerned with therapy, enlightenment, harmonising inner forces. The forces that are aroused in the East are elevated and balanced in the South. In this Quarter we find the gods of redemption, the great Saviours and enlighteners of humanity. We also find the midsummer gods of the land who bring the highest solar forces to bear upon the earth within the turning of the wheel of the year. The implement of the South is the Rod or Staff.

West

In the West we find gods of maturity, of Autumn, fruitfulness, giving, generosity, plenty. The Element is Water, and the gods of transit, the ferrymen, the subtle changers and gentle teachers are found here. The potent water gods of the ancestral world are here, both as deities of the rivers, oceans, and as local guardians of springs and wells. The cosmic tides of space and time are the higher octave of this Quarter, and so we also find gods of universal love and compassion, the transformative and enabling powers of the spirit in the ocean of Being. The implement of the West is the Cup.

North

In the North we find gods of old age, of winter, of death. The Element is Earth, and the old gods are not weak or negative, but filled with the strength of the earth. The higher octaves of this Quarter are those of wisdom, of readiness, and calm. It leads to the realisation of the night sky and stars. Paradoxically the earth-gods are also the star gods. Here also are the gods of sleep, peace, rest, forgetting, and final transition from one world to another. Ancestral teachers and guides are found in the North, the gods that communicate wisdom and offer it to us as practical guidance. The implement of the North is the Shield or Mirror.

In mythic cycles, we often find that a hero or god travels around the Wheel, changing with the seasons. At Spring he is newly born, filled with the rush and inspiration of life. At Summer he becomes an adult, holding his peak of power on balance and harmony. By Autumn he has become the mature man, the giver. At Winter he is old and wise, often becoming a teacher. At the transition between North and East, he dies, to be reborn again upon a further turning of the Wheel.

Above

This is the realm of the stars, and the eternal depths of the universe. There is a paradoxical relationship between above and below, which is adequately highlighted by modern theories of relativity. In a general sense, the Direction Above is that of Ultimate Divinity - this may be the Sky Father in a simple world model, or it may be universal Being.

Below

This is the realm of the Underworld, which paradoxically holds the stars. The Direction Below is that of the Earth Mother, or more universally of the Great Mother of all Being. Above and below can be inverted or reverted at any time, and some very powerful magical techniques consist of exactly this process.

Within

Within is the living spirit, the core or seed of Being. This may manifest to the imagination in innumerable ways: for men it is often the primal Child of Light, eternal, unchanging, radiant. At its deepest level the Direction Within touches upon the Source, the utterance of Being out of silence. All Directions, Gods, Goddesses, stars planets and zones are within, but to merely state this in words is insufficient, a set of phrases that leads us away from proper contemplation or experience.

7

The King Within

Kingship is associated with the heart or heart centre of consciousness and energy. This is the point of poise that harmonises all energies. The King mediates between the Land (the worker, body or feet) and the Stars (priest, spirit, or head). The King may also partake of all or any Branch; Divine or Sacred Kings were, in theory if not always in practice, individuals with a fully developed conscious fusion between the Branches of Priest and King. Whatever such Kings enacted for the Land and the people was directly inspired or attuned to spiritual power.

In personal terms the King or central harmonising potential brings the often conflicting energies and motives of our inner Warrior, Poet, Priest, and Prophet into a proper relationship to one another. Very often this has to be worked through by encountering each Branch until they are balanced with one another. Kingship tends to come after years of developing skills and inner energies through emphasis on other Branches. Very often Kingship is realised by working upon one's weakest Branch, rather than constantly building upon innate abilities confined within one specific Branch.

The Sacred Kingship

Voluntary incarnation is the first sacrifice.
The sacrificial life is the second.
The sacrificial death is the third.

The Male Mysteries cannot be discussed, approached or brought alive for the future without some understanding of the major Branch of the Sacred Kingship. There is no claim here, in this book, or by the author, to completely understand or to present this Branch of the Mysteries in full or in any so-called 'authoritative' manner.

The Sacred Kingship opens out many levels of understanding, many realms of awareness, and no particular individual or school can truthfully lay claim to it. Those that do so, be they single teachers, orders, cults, or world religions, are either deluded or intentionally lying. Delusion and illusion are unavoidable (but not irredeemable) conditions of our collective humanity; but intentional lies regarding spiritual or liberating truths are powerful vehicles of manifest evil and corruption. No single spiritual path to truth and liberation has been so lavishly convolutedly and persistently enmeshed in lies as that of the Sacred Kingship.

Before we begin to examine the Sacred Kingship it must be stated that not all men enter this Branch of the Male Mysteries, and that there is no 'requirement' that any individual should do so. Nevertheless, any male wishing to develop through the esoteric traditions and the Five Branches must have some understanding of the Sacred Kingship, as membership of this Mystery may be realised at any time, often under the most surprising or unexpected circumstances. Furthermore, the work of all the other Branches is connected in a harmonic fashion to that of the Sacred Kingship, just as each Branch is interconnected harmonically with the rest.

The Sacred Kingship, however, is the deepest or central Branch of the Male Mysteries in the human world. Many aspects of esoteric training, development, and the enablement and transfer of inner energies and spiritual powers, centralise and focus within and from the Sacred Kingship.

Much has been written on the subject, ranging from anthropological studies of human sacrifice through to refined theology in an orthodox and carefully controlled context. There is a wide rift between a historical viewpoint of the Sacred Kingship in various primal cultures and early civilisations, and the inner condition or Mystery as a living power. This rift is due to the long-term effect of orthodox political Christianity, which strove to subsume or destroy all branches of the Mysteries, and to erase all other cults and religions which it saw, and still sees today, as actual or potential rivals.

Esoterically we learn that early, or what we might truthfully call primal, Christianity, before the cult was corrupted by political aims and lust for world domination, was based upon the ancient and widespread Mystery of the Sacrificial or Sacred Kingship. To this extent it was, on the surface, little different from a number of other sacrificial cults that seed, rise, and decay, within the overall ground of human religion through the ages.

There is, however, a wealth of spiritual and magical lore concerning the degree or octave of realisation afforded by the sacrifice of Jesus of Nazareth, and his relationship to the consciousness of the solar system, the universe, and ultimate Being. We may set aside, at this stage, any discussion as to the possible truth or falsehood of such esoteric lore; this endless type of argument leads us nowhere other than into the hands of manipulators of dogma and suppression. The degree of truth and falsehood in any inner, transpersonal, fundamental matter of consciousness and entity, is always relative, and must be based upon experience rather than theory or dogma.

Most of the 'rival' cults, including those more primal forms of Christianity itself, rooted into the perennial religions and wisdom traditions of our world, were forced underground by ruthless persecution of variant sects during the early days of the developing political Christianity, particularly after its adoption as a state religion by the late Roman Empire. The esoteric teachings, however, still exist undamaged, and may be regained or regenerated by certain techniques of altered consciousness.

The underground traditions tended to preserve such techniques and perpetuate them, rather than preserve detailed sets of beliefs, instructions, or information itself. Information without perception or understanding is, needless to say, of no value whatsoever. As time passed and historical or material oppression increased from state religion, it became less and less viable to preserve rigidly detailed sets of alternative beliefs. Much lore was preserved in the dream-like state of the collective imagination, and in folk tradition, rooted into national or tribal and environmental forms. The esoteric techniques, however, were handed down through personal instruction, or through regeneration within traditional forms. More simply, the techniques cause the inner truths and teachings to regenerate within the individual imagination. There was, therefore, no need to preserve dogma or rigid sets of so-called facts, these were the tools of suppressive state religion in any case.

In our present context we need to be aware, first, that true or inner Christianity is a quite different matter from the aggressive male-stereotypical political religion of outer history. Inner, primal, or esoteric Christianity, is based firmly within the ancient Mystery, the Great Goddess and the Sacred Kingship.

An older precedent within the orthodox Judaeo-Christian texts, pre-dating that of the sacrifice of Jesus, is that of *Melchizadek*, an Old Testament figure deriving from the ancient (pagan) Sacred Kingship practices in the Middle East. One of the most powerful streams of consciousness in the Male Mysteries is known as the Order of Melchizadek, with various expressions ranging from highly orthodox to underground and long-secret fusions of pagan Gnostic and primal Christian tradition, teaching, and esoteric arts and sciences.

We shall return to this Order of Melchizadek later. At this stage, however, it must be stated that the use of the Old Testament example, that of Melchizadek, King of Salem, does not, and never has, limited the consciousness and energy of the Mystery to a Judaeo-Christian context. We shall explore this complex but not insoluble paradox shortly.

The Sacred Kingship is a holism, an inter-resonating pattern of energy and consciousness, enfolding and generating various entities ranging from human to transhuman or divine. Such entities live within one another; they have a constant interaction upon one another; the interaction is timeless, and defies the accepted or habitual barriers of space, physical entity, and energy. Did we but know it, we are all within such states or entities of holism or interaction, male and female. Such is the nature of our environment, our planet, our universe. There are holisms within holisms, and the thresholds between such collectives are thresholds of energy: for human and other self-conscious entities, these thresholds mark changes of awareness.

Many of the more subtle levels of interaction are only consciously realised and fully enabled through radical changes of awareness, and through changes of the flow-patterns or cycles of our vital energies. Through such changes or realignments, time, space, and habitual energy patterns are altered, inverted, even altogether obviated and disposed of. In the magical and spiritual arts and disciplines, such changes are generated through work with specific training programmes. Such training programmes involve the fusion of physical, mental, and imaginative techniques with concepts and images. One of the results or transformation sought is that of relationships formed with spiritual or innerworld beings. These beings are the spirits, gods, goddesses, and other such entities of religion, myth, and esoteric tradition. The entire subject of divine beings, and the literal or symbolic nature of gods and goddesses is discussed elsewhere in this book so we shall temporarily bypass it here.

When we examine the Sacred Kingship, we have a historical picture, well known from many early cultures, involving literal kingship and literal sacrifice, making a cycle of connections between the human and transhuman or divine worlds and dimensions. But in a modern context this background is merely representative of the manifestation of the Mystery upon a collective level in human life. The kingship, its sacred quality, and the acts of sacrifice are ultimately inner personal and transpersonal events. Such events work in a different manner for males than for females. Men and women each play equal roles in the Mysteries, and these roles are far different from the dreary stereotypes of masculinity and femininity that still permeate our culture today as a result of propaganda and long-term programmes of mass conditioning and suppression. There is no suggestion here that the spiritual sacrificial volunteers are inevitably men, this is not the case. There is, however, an extensive tradition of men being sacrificed, which has its roots in very early matriarchal and Goddess-worshipping cultures. The predominance of men as Sacred Kings, as spiritual sacrifices, or in similar roles, is not, and never has been, any part of the stereotype of 'male superiority'.

Modern genetics seems to mirror, upon a microcosmic, microscopic level, the same pattern that is found in the Mystery - the male unit is, somehow, disposable after he has performed certain functions within the collective being. But that is only part of the picture, for if we limit it to a materialist level, then it is a most unbalanced pattern indeed. The sacrificed or disposable male entity, be it a cell, a sperm, a genetic fragment, or a human, is reborn again and again. Thus the life of the 'sacrificed' male is not a line that terminates, but a spiral , or even a spiral of spirals.

In the context of the Male Mysteries, therefore, we need to discover why men are sacrificed, and why women, traditionally, mediate certain functions and aspects of the sacrifice. This spiritual and magical teaching is, fortunately, fully defined in the perennial traditions, though in a number of variant presentations. Such understanding only comes from experience on a number of levels of consciousness, and not from simply learning lists of attributes or the details of an illustration.

We need also to be endlessly vigilant, to guard against confusing the transpersonal truths of the Mysteries with the simple therapeutic realisations of modern psychology. There are many levels of consciousness to the Sacred Kingship which are unknown in psychotherapy. We may stay with this important difference for the present, and consider briefly one of the great initiatory changes of consciousness found in esoteric disciplines and training, and its very unique manifestation through the Mystery of the Sacred Kingship.

In all magical traditions worldwide, there is a level of awareness concerning ancestral contact. This may be rationalised through modern genetics, or through the Jungian concept of the collective unconscious, but no matter what terminology we use, direct communication with the Ancestors is a reality of esoteric initiation. The major difference between this type of connection in the esoteric traditions and in modern genetics or psychology is that the initiate experiences the awareness *consciously*, and not through a scientific or intellectual model or in any other interface designed in a theoretical or experimental manner.[10]

In the Mystery of the Sacred Kingship, this shared consciousness, this diffusion of collective experience through time and space, is, contrary to the usual manner of collective traditions and consciousness, not genetically dependent. Initiation into the Mystery gives the individual a conscious sharing, a direct contact with the memories and transpersonal modes of awareness of those who have gone before within the Mystery. The many individuals concerned need not be related genetically, and need not have any lines of ancestral connectivity.

This potential is found in the source text from Judaic or Semitic tradition, as to the nature of Melchizadek who was 'without father or mother'. It may also be referred to the obscure sayings of Jesus of Nazareth concerning the separation of spiritual enlightenment from family ties.

Part Three

~

Visualisations and Exercises

8

Visualising Transformation

The exercises in this book are modern developments, unique to the author, but they are broadly based upon the perennial traditions, techniques and teachings of the Western Mysteries. With this foundation they derive from a coherent and enduring tradition of spiritual transformation, preserved and actively taught in the West for thousands of years. The traditional techniques for transformation and empowerment may take a variety of forms, and work through several different schools or lines of contact. In this book, of course, we are dealing specifically with a restatement of the Male Mysteries, so material relating to men is given a special emphasis. The Mysteries, however, are for men and women equally, and the Male and Female Mysteries ultimately unite together. There are times and places where men and women need to work separately, and times and places where they need to work together. The western esoteric tradition, being a universal source of spiritual transformation, provides ample working material for all such situations phases or levels of consciousness.

There is no need, however, for the individual man or group wishing to use the new exercises offered here to become deeply absorbed in the western esoteric tradition, or to study it in depth. The basic exercises can be attempted straight away with no background study or preliminary work. Indeed, they often work more effectively if no preconceptional or intellectual work has been done beforehand.

When these exercises are taken at face value, and honestly attempted, they inevitably produce definite results. They are designed to work on their own, relating to one another through the patterns of relationship described in our various chapters and shown in our illustrations. Some basic skill at visualising and meditation will be very helpful when you begin the work, but if you have no previous experience in these disciplines, do not be put off. They will work anyway, but the less experienced visualiser or meditator may only become aware of their effect slowly; in some cases, where there are severe blocks upon the imagination, a calm repeated effort is necessary to free up the inner faculties.

Occasionally the freedom will come through a cathartic or explosive reaction, which unblocks the individual suddenly, leaving a clear perception and sense of returning to a reality and level of consciousness that had almost been lost. This last experience is a common one, particularly for men who have lived for years on false values of assertiveness and merit, and have lost touch with their inner nature as a result. These exercises can give considerable help in rebalancing us when we are in the rigid unnatural states still required, even demanded, of men in western society.

One of the open secrets of esoteric or spiritual methods of self-transformation is that they are very simple. Everyone assumes that something powerful must be complex or even tedious, but this is untrue. Any of the basic visualisations in this book may be taken at face value, as a simple event involving images, framed within a basic narrative or story-telling, and a period of stillness in private. If they are worked in this manner they will produce results that are clear, powerful, and often surprising.

For many centuries, the hidden traditions required that extensive training take place, and that no student should work with powerful visualisations or god and goddess-forms until they had undergone a basic course in various disciplines. This requirement is not, as is often assumed, based upon secrecy or elitism, but upon common sense. It is designed to protect the student from accidents, and to build his or her abilities gradually. It still holds good for many of the techniques of ritual magic, advanced visualisation, and related arts and disciplines, but the base-line, or threshold of initiation, has altered somewhat in the twentieth century.

During the last twenty years, (1970-1990) there has been a gradual raising of consciousness and a slow but definite change of collective imagination in the West. No one should pretend that this is a widespread dawning of mass illumination, but it is clear that people are beginning to pay more attention to inner arts and disciplines. Partly as a result of the increased number of meditators, visualisers, and partly as a result of deep changes of collective consciousness which have occurred, it is possible to offer attuned and powerful visualisations and exercises for almost immediate use. It is also possible to know that many people will be able to work with them.

Visualisation, Exercises and Energies

Three distinct paths or broadly defined methods of working with inner energies can be easily distinguished. As a general rule we tend to combine these in varying ways, though they can each be exclusively developed as specific systems of training. Examples of each are found throughout the world.

The first is physical use of the body. Movement, posture, and polarity working (such as sexual activity) can arouse and transform life energies. Techniques such as yoga, tai-chi, warrior skills and arts, dance, and ritual movement or polarity work of any physical sort, are all examples of this path.

The second is through personal meditation and concentration. In such techniques the meditator focuses upon the inner energies and brings them through consciously, whereas they had previously been dormant or automatic and unconscious. This path includes many techniques of conscious or willed arousal of our individual power-centres (chakras), and those vast traditions of spiritual and mystical meditation and contemplation in which the individual passes within to increasingly deeper levels of being, until the inner power or divinity is met. The life-power or divinity is, in the latter stages of such work, consciously brought out to transform the entire entity, and then to flow or radiate to the outer world.

The third path is that of imagery, visualisation, and the use of god- and goddess-forms. This is the way of the magical primal and mythic or religious traditions, and is probably the least understood and least practised today. Upon this path, the individual or group does not necessarily focus upon inner energies directly, but encounters living images or innerworld beings. These are usually defined through a mythic structure as gods, goddesses, or as transcendent or underworld beings, often closely linked to the land or to elemental forces in nature.

The encountering and exchange of energies within such visualisations and meetings has a distinct effect upon the individual, and will act very deeply indeed in some cases. Thereafter he or she may be able to draw consciously upon energies that were previously blocked or dormant. Many of the primal magical shamanistic and sophisticated magical arts depend upon such meetings. There is a vast store of half-obscured knowledge concerning the procedures, and individual traditions rely upon meetings with specific beings, such as ancestors, spiritual animals, gods and goddesses, and innerworld teachers. In specific traditions the same entities may persist for thousands of years virtually unchanged, or may manifest through variant forms according to cultural changes. The simplest way of defining this path is to regard it as a highly amplified and accelerated variant of the life-cycle, and of our usual growth through encounters with other people and ensuing transformational experiences.

It is for this reason that such techniques frequently use the Wheel of Life (Figure 1), which shows the resonance and holism between the Four Elements, the Four Seasons, the Directions, and the human life cycle. Specific transformative and initiatory or teaching entities are located in different Quarters of the Circle, and we progress around it or towards them by highly energised means in visualisation and ritual pattern making. This type of work was central to the ancient Mysteries, and can be startlingly effective in modern use.

Visualising the Future

Meditation has received considerable popular attention in the last twenty years, though there are a number of quite different interpretations of what, exactly, meditation is and what the meditator's aims and methods, if any, should be. Such interpretations range from those embedded within religious or spiritual traditions, such as yogic, Hindu, Buddhist, or Christian meditation, all being effective methods yet quite distinct from one another, to generalised techniques of many varieties. Such generalised techniques, widely found in the New Age movement, vary considerably; some of the popular types would not strictly seem to be meditation at all but consciously induced daydream or reverie. Perennial and esoteric or magical arts employ very precise techniques of meditation, usually embedded within little-known traditions and schools of inner development.

Visualisation has, until recently, been given less popular prominence, but is now used in various schools of general meditation, therapy, and for a range of what would traditionally be considered spurious reasons such as 'getting what you want'. This commercial aspect of using visualisation to obtain desired ends, is now widely sold in popular books and tapes. It is a typical example of our modern fragmentary techniques of accessing or altering consciousness, too often used in abnormal and potentially damaging contexts.

Yes, we can get what we want through visualisation; this simple fact has been known for millennia, but there is a large risk of this 'wanting' backfiring on us. There is a simple but profound teaching in the western tradition, which was restated by the late Dion Fortune as 'Be careful what you ask for, as you are very likely to receive it.'[11] How many times have we all regretted asking for something in every day life, wishing for something, or someone, to happen to us, and then, after our wish has been granted, saying 'If only I'd known...' To seek apparent benefit from our wishes, we should first know what we really want. Knowing what we want should then be related to what we truly need, and at some point after this, we may indeed gain some insight into a balanced target for certain types of wish-fulfilling visualisation.

The esoteric traditions use visualisation in a quite different way, usually in the context of a mythic or collective framework, and in practice tied into very specific images or holisms of imagery and energy. The perennial wisdom traditions worldwide have always taught that *whatever we want transforms us until we want it no longer.* This truth is employed in magical ritual, and in meditation and visualisation, using images and what seem to be defined goals and ends purely for the transformative effect that they have. When these transformative acts are undertaken, we usually cannot know in full what effect they might have - they are often leaps in the dark. Traditional teachings, however, when sensibly assessed, provide certain general but significant guidelines as to how the techniques work, and where they often (but not inevitably) lead.

No man who longs and strives to become a master can ever succeed in his wish. If he does achieve liberation he finds that the mastery which he sought is now behind him or, as is more commonly experienced, that it is ever beyond him - it is a means and not an end.

The conflict between what we think we want, what we have been forced or conditioned to want, and what the deeper often masked or blocked resonances of ourselves may want, can be devastating. Sometimes not one of these apparent wants, at any accessible level, will be harmonious to our deepest or spiritual needs. Here is a vast area which materialist psychology cannot address or assist the individual; when the spiritual impetus directs or seeks a course totally counter to the conditions or habits of life. Such deep utterances of our essential being cannot be addressed or resolved by mental therapy, but must be experienced in full, even if they lead to terrible and outwardly irresolvable situations.

Fortunately for most of us this degree of spiritual impetus or volition is rare. We usually receive it second-hand, so to speak, from the resonance of the lives of great spiritual mediators, teachers, saints, heroes and heroines. Such people, male and female,,are not necessarily limited to the world's roll-call of prominent historical or cult characters with claims to spiritual status - many are anonymous, some are reviled, but their impetus remains. This important theme is discussed in Chapter 7 on the Sacred Kingship.

The problem of relating want and need is often bitterly experienced by modern men, who are, even when aware of the problem, in despite of themselves, conditioned to achieving goals, making grades, gaining obvious and formalised merits, essentially confusing greed with need. Many men, of course, are not aware of any problem, only of a dimly felt but incurable inner conflict and tension, which is increased rather than alleviated by gaining, striving and apparently succeeding. The modern phenomenon of stress, manifesting widely in both men and women, is one obvious yet frustratingly elusive and insoluble illness deriving from inner conflict with outer situations and circumstances.

The individual male is often under a heavy pressure to seek so-called security in outer forms such as status, possessions, appearance, popularity and so forth. This applies also to development of skills, egocentric competitiveness, sexual gratification and fame. Very few people, men or women, turn about and ask where this pressure comes from. Only when we begin to do so does it begin to fade, for it is an illusion that perpetuates itself only through acceptance; it consists of energy misaligned and misplaced. It should be stated firmly, however, that the original misalignments, albeit of a different nature to their expression today, were quite intentional, seeded in the culture through a religious psychology of spiritual, mental and emotional control. Western society was literally imagined or *imaged* into its present state of vicious imbalance and self destruction. It only needed our greed to follow, and of course we are all and always greedy.

In (approximately) the 1950s visualisation was 'discovered', through an unfortunate fusion of an assorted ragbag of consciousness-transforming techniques and popular psychology. It was loudly hailed as a guaranteed means of gaining nebulous materialist ends such as wealth and indomitable will-power. For the last forty years it has been given numerous purchasable presentations, ranging from cheap paperback books to very expensive courses presented to clients in exclusive surroundings.

Visualisation has also been used widely in alternative therapies. Certain visualising techniques involving colour, scenarios or dream-like locations, occasionally linked to specific music, are essentially loose fragments from the perennial spiritual and esoteric traditions of altering consciousness. Many modern therapeutic techniques can be traced directly to spiritualism and

Theosophical Society origins in the nineteenth century, even though they are now used in a purely materialist context such as psychotherapy or alternative treatment for stress or incurable disease. Strictly speaking the best cure for many of the imbalances treated by such alternative methods is to cure the vicious society and the inner and outer pollution that causes such illnesses, rather than concentrate, however compassionately, effectively or validly, upon individual manifestations. But this global cure would, of course, be too idealist and unprofitable.

Before we proceed with visualisations relevant to the Male Mysteries, it is well worth reassessing the function and effect of visualisation. Even if you are familiar with or experienced in visualisation, this short reassessment may be valuable in the context of the specific visualisations in this book.

Why Visualise?

Why visualise? First, we need to be aware that conscious visualisation, as a specific exercise, is only a development of a mode of awareness that we experience ceaselessly. The imagination, our image making capacity of consciousness, works continuously, though often upon a subliminal level or below a threshold that we seldom consciously cross. Visualisation involves steering the imagination through conscious adaptation and controlled generation of chosen sets of images: but it does not remain at that initial level, as anyone working with the exercises in this book will discover.

Our imagination today is focused and consciously engaged through media such as reading, music, drama, radio, and to a lesser extent, film, and to an even lesser extent through television. As a general rule the more obviously detailed and specific a series of *externalised* images is (such as television where visual images are externalised upon a very small surface) the less stimulus they provide for the imagination. No comment or general criticism is being passed here on relative merits or quality (this is a different discussion altogether), merely upon the simple effects of certain media upon the imagination, regardless of the content of the material that they convey.

The visual arts, of course, can provide exceptions to this general rule of externalised imagery, for such arts are, or should be, inspired from very deep levels of perception and intuition. This inspiration is then embodied in the work of art, and resonates to any person experiencing it.

The imagination atrophies if it is not used. Widespread television has resulted in a substantial lowering of our individual and collective image-making abilities. Curiously, when the imagination atrophies, so does the memory, the length of attention-span, and many other aspects of consciousness. It is as if the holism of human consciousness is energised by the imagination. We shall return to this possibility shortly.

Concentrated image-making as a deliberate controlled activity is, even without the degenerative effect of our modern toys and entertainments, very rare. We are perhaps more familiar today with random image-making in the association processes that are highlighted and used in modern psychotherapy. We need to be absolutely clear, however, that free-association and similar random association methods were not used in the esoteric traditions. Under some circumstances, such as heightened consciousness or in highly energised groups or powerful geomantic sites and sacred locations, free association and random drifting can be detrimental to the individual - the inner equivalent of wandering idly across a busy motorway.

Ancient Visions: Modern Applications

To realise where the magical or perennial spiritual traditions of visualisation come from, we must consider collective myth-making and poetry or story-telling. This is where the imagination is discovered to be the energising source for other expressions or modes of awareness; the memory, the power of attention and concentration, and the higher consciousness of empathy, compassion and spiritual liberation.

Historically we find that mythic lore was embodied in long poems and tales. Some of the great mythic epics took not hours but days to tell, furthermore, people truly listened to them, retold them, and held them within their minds and imaginations as an integral part of their lives. Such concepts seem almost impossible to us today, yet they are still present in potential in every human being. Furthermore, primal peoples in isolated regions today sing long epic ballads, tell long tales, and consciously relate such mythic material to the creation of their land, their ancestors, and on initiatory levels, to magical and spiritual transformation and empowerment. It is these levels of imagination that need to be restored and employed in any modern equivalent or restatement of the Mysteries, be it for men, women, individuals, or groups. Anything less is merely an intellectual exercise or a fabrication with no living source.

Clearly there is little point in expecting modern men and women to learn epic tales, dances and dramas relating the creation of the world or worlds. In any case, we do not live according to the social patterns in which such mythic lore was created and preserved. But we still have the elements of this lore within us, for creation myth and certain key images are both preserved and regenerated at the deepest levels of our consciousness, our entity, our being.[12] The old magical and spiritual traditions encapsulated their collective diffuse mythic lore into very precise sets of images, into god and goddess forms, and into certain key patterns and tales, used both in visualisation and in ritual dance or ceremonial magic.

If we seek to transform ourselves, visualisation is one of the most potent tools for such transformation. Once the imaging faculty has been awakened, and this is surprisingly easy for most of us, it draws to itself and empowers many other aspects of consciousness and energy. The imagination is very closely linked to our sexual energies; we might say that they are apparently polarised manifestations of the same life and death forces that reside within us all.

The more advanced techniques in traditional magical arts or spiritual meditation and visualisation always involve our sexual energies, though not necessarily in any physically gratifying activity. The sexual energies, called the *Inner Fire* in the western traditions, are aroused by imagination, but the imagery need not be, and in practice seldom is, 'sexual' as modern people understand sexuality. The popular delusions, frequently published in the gutter press, of magical arts involving orgies, forced physical sex, or unusual physical sexual acts are simply generated by wishful thinking, but they are also perpetuated and inflamed by commercial and religious vested interests.

It is interesting to note that the most repellent and unnatural acts are always voiced (when accusing other religions, pagans, magicians, and so forth) by people in fundamental religious movements. They seem to need to accuse others of whatever they themselves hide in their most foul fantasies. Or perhaps this is too harsh a judgement, and they are merely so insecure in their own beliefs that they need to find negative images of other peoples' ways and worship to reassure themselves in moments of doubt and despair. Compassion has no place in such fundamentalist nightmares, so, inevitably, the regenerative purifying energy of the imagination is never allowed to unfold.

Strength and Falling Towers

It does not take long to realise, even upon an intellectual level, that imagination and visualisation may be used for positive liberating ends, or for negative suppressive ends. Ironically, most people, male and female, use their divine power of imaging to imprison themselves, even to degrade themselves. Once the imagination and sexual energies become linked in a cycle or loop of negative implication and effect, it requires special effort to suspend such patterns and break away from them. By special effort we need not mean strenuous effort, or prolonged therapy. Many of the specific visualisations found in the Mysteries will undertake this task for us - not necessarily as a prime effect, but merely through their inevitable realignment of our innermost energies.

Very often, in matters of consciousness and energy, if we set out to visualise or meditate with a specific end in mind, we defeat that end, or reinforce its opposite tendency within ourselves. Traditional methods, however, involve imagery and energies, usually associated with ancient divine entities, that empower but initially break down our conditioned inner constructs, patterns, habits, and addictions. Such constructs exist upon at least two levels; the collective or human holism, and the individual level which accumulates in one lifetime. In the esoteric traditions we learn that there are also resonances and patterns of energy carried over from previous lives. This is, perhaps, the simplest way of stating the greatly misrepresented and misunderstood 'laws' of reincarnation and karma.

The breaking down of patterns is, in itself, not too difficult to achieve. There is an increasing move towards implementing such psychic breakdown in alternative therapies and group work loosely based upon primal traditions; but because the cathartic or catabolic breaking-down is easy to induce, and because the balancing, anabolic or building training and imagery take years for a conscientious teacher or guide to acquire and use effectively, there can be problems. Once again (as previously discussed) we find that problems arise because cathartic techniques are nowadays taken out of their proper life context and spiritual or transformative tradition, and used diffusely in the therapeutic or experiential modern group. This borrowing is often not, in itself, enough to fully regenerate or liberate us.

Visualising is one of the more obviously definable manifestations of our well-spring of life and energy; this is exactly why the imagination and the sexual energies and habits are so closely intertwined. If we are truly able to visualise we can change not only ourselves, but the form and manifestation of the world around us. This concept is at the foundation of ritual magic; the word magic is a close relative of the word imagination - imaging in or out from the source of Being.

When confronted with this proposition, most people assume hat it takes truly titanic amounts of effort, energy, will-power and discipline to re-route their habits of imagination. This would be true, if we were to attempt to serially and literally recondition all that has arisen and patterned itself within us during our entire lives to the present moment. But massive application of will-power and effort are frequently counter-productive; they are often associated with the overkill that is typical to the male delusion of riding rough-shod over problems, cutting through knots, heaving boulders from the path and so forth. This delusion is by no means confined exclusively to men, though it is often stated to be a typically male attitude. At present it is deeply rooted in the habits and language of our culture, and so effects both men and women, particularly those in a position of power. The scale of such power ranges from personal relationships to world economics and politics.

We are not so much individuals upon blocked paths, but the very paths and boulders themselves. We have to roll ourselves away to be reborn, rather than think that some technique, master, bought-in salvation, or exclusive religion will do it for us.

Curiously we find this truth stated in the most modern of sciences, that of computer prediction through complex mathematical models. In recent years scientists have realised that even in the most materialist of mathematical models, the beating of a bird's wing in an isolated forest can and does effect our global weather. That which is powerful, as the mystical traditions have always taught, is that which is very slight, imperceptible, and yet which permeates all. If Alexander the Great had known exactly where and when to sneeze, rather than draw his sharp keen sword, the Gordian Knot would have unravelled completely - even if our hero had been thousands of milcs distant from it.

In tarot, two trumps reveal this truth: the Blasted Tower and Strength. Both emblems feature also in mythic or spiritual traditions that predate the appearance of tarot cards, and have their counterparts in the legends and literature of world religion. The Blasted Tower is a construct unnaturally held together and upright by force, long after it should have reached a state of collapse and decay leading to regeneration. The image is usually one of a show of power and despotic will being blasted and destroyed by natural (i.e. divine) forces. The polar opposite or partner is Strength, in which a savage primal beast, usually a lion, is shown under the imperceptible yet certain control of a gentle maiden. In some modern decks this has been altered into a male strong-man such as Hercules wrestling the beast down, but to do so totally cuts the image off from its deep roots and its true meaning. When such emblems are seen in pairs, or more subtly, in triads and quaternities, they begin to fully work for us.[13]

Visualisation realigns our energies; they are carried along with and through the pattern or story of the visualisation, and emerge beyond it transformed, regenerated, and often greatly empowered or amplified. But because they are transformed, many of our notions of so-called power are lost en-route. It is quite likely that if we are to seek spiritual masters and men of power in the outer world, that they exist in the most obvious and unnoticed places. They are certainly not supermen living in special communities or in isolated parts of the planet. A master, assuming he existed at all, would consider such self-indulgence to be weakness indeed. Why be superhuman when you could, instead, be free? But the true spiritual traditions go even further, and say why be free when your fellow humans are still enslaved? There can be no elite or elect in a whole world, in a pleroma or full universe.

Visualisation: The Basic Methods of Visualising

1. A period of calm, of stillness and simple meditation is first undertaken to clarify consciousness. This may be unified with rhythmic breathing, and should be done with eyes closed. Do not use complex prayers, chants, mantrams and so forth, even if you are used to working with these. The aim is to simply still and prepare the imagination for the visualisation which is to follow. (Appendix 1 is a modern version of a traditional ancient method for approaching Silence.)

2. A chosen narrative and sequence of images is then built in your imagination, either through someone reading or reciting the imagery aloud (if you are working in a group), or from a pre-recorded tape if you are working alone. The visualisations can also be learned by working with pre-recorded tapes, and expanded by pausing the tape for silent work when necessary. This last method is a very productive way of using modern technology for inner development.[14]

Another well-proven method is to read the visualisation aloud to yourself several times, until you begin know it well. Then begin to work with it in silent visualisation with eyes closed. You will find that far from being a laborious test of memory, the images come through easily. It is quite acceptable to work with eyes closed but the text open on your lap; if, in the early stages, you falter, simply open your eyes and read the passage aloud to yourself; then return to working with closed eyes, building the images as clearly as possible. You will soon be able to work without the text.

The secret of this technique lies in *not* attempting to learn each visualisation as a test of memory, but simply to read it aloud to yourself until you are familiar with it. During the readings, you will gradually build the sequence into your imagination; the mind remembers repeated sequences heard and told aloud far more readily than it does material from the printed page.

This deep memory is particularly enhanced when we use magical or archetypical imagery and narratives. Such techniques have been active for thousands of years, and may be traced historically to cultures such as ancient Greece and Egypt, which used such mythic narratives in religion, in training for priests and priestesses, and in the Mysteries. The historical ambience of a magical or spiritual technique, however, is merely a series of surface connections; on deeper levels far more is discovered by our actual practice than can ever be researched or described intellectually.

The Relative Merits of Each Method

There are quite distinct advantages and possible disadvantages to each of the methods described, and each will produce varying results and potentials within the overall framework of any visualisation. Let us consider each method briefly:

1. Pre-recorded Tapes

The use of tapes gives a regular rhythm and structure to the visualisations; they may be enhanced by special music which is usually an aid to imaginative work (providing it does not become a distraction or a habitual prop). The disadvantages of tapes are most likely to be connected to dependence. It is very important that we do not become dependent upon a technological aid towards changing consciousness, so we should not fall into the habit of visualising or meditating solely to a pre-recorded sequence of words or music. Tapes may eventually seem too rigid and predefined after some practice, but some aspects of this problem may be obviated by using a pause switch.

2. Group Work With a Reader or Reciter

Once again, the structure is defined by the voice of the reader, who steers the sequence for the visualisers. An experienced visualiser can work while reading a text aloud, and a really good group guide will work entirely from memory. This gives the opportunity to pace and vary the silent periods, or in the case of advanced work, to improvise certain sections of the visualisations.

The disadvantages are that it is by no means easy to find a competent reader. A mutually supportive group will take it in turns to read, to ensure that there is no 'star' or 'leader' status building up; this is especially important for men in group work, as there are many undercurrents of striving and seeking after false authority that are carried over from outer life.

Another difficult area in reading aloud in group work is the judgement of the improvised sections. There is sometimes a tendency for the reader to wander off into increasingly vague and disconnected visions, losing the focus of the main visualisation. The key to successful visualisation is to always remain within the guidelines of the main imagery, and not to depart too far from it. Departures may be individual during the silent phases, which are then reattuned when the main sequence begins again. If departures are led by the reader or reciter, he or she must always return to the main sequence, bringing it fully through to its predefined conclusion.

Originally all empowering visualisations were worked in this manner, ranging from epic poetry and story-telling, to the highly specialised use of magical images such as god- and goddess-forms in spiritual and magical training. Old tales and songs that were used as fireside entertainment frequently held a deeper level, which was available to those who wished to know.

The status attached to the role of poet, bard, or storyteller in early cultures is not simply one of crude entertainment. The bard was a vessel through which all knowledge, all images and paths to realisation, could flow. His or her memory preserved the history of the people, and could draw upon a vast store of mythic and genealogical lore to educate, initiate, and bind a people together.

3. Reading Aloud to Yourself

Reading aloud to yourself and eventually learning the visualisation can be a slow process, but is very effective. Once again, the danger lies in drifting off the main sequence, and the temptation to indulge in freeform fantasy rather then defined visualisation. The two are very different in their effect, and as a rule free fantasy is not used in the Mysteries. The method is such that once our imagination has been attuned by the images, then a period of free visualisation will always work with the attuned imagery. Free fantasy is a lower or lesser use of the imagination, empowered visualisation is a higher form and definition of our inner energies.

In Appendix 3 you will find a detailed narrative visualisation for encountering one of the major god-forms, that of the Guardian or Horned God, also known as Pan or Cernunnos. This is not a matter of paganism or ancient god revival, but of a power and image inherent in the human consciousness, both male and female. The visualisation given, with detailed notes, is based upon a type of imagery that has endured for many centuries in the underground or vestigial Mystery systems and the initiations of folk or chthonic practices. Once preserved solely by tales and songs, such visions may be redefined for modern use by expanded narratives. This visualisation should be used to supplement our work programme described in the following chapters, and may be undertaken at any time.

9

Gods and Visions

Essentially magic is a collection of arts and primal sciences reaching far back into ancestral beliefs and practices, but slowly being updated and reassessed within each century. It is based simply upon the use of the human imagination and associated vital energies to interact with other energies, entities, and images. It permeates religion, art, music, folklore and tradition. In the ancient world magic was the source of sophisticated and powerful techniques of inner transformation, therapy, and held a detailed understanding of human psychology in both mythic and metaphysical terms.

A great proportion of magic is holistic, concerned with the wholeness and interrelationship of living creatures and the land and planet. Due to nineteenth-century intellectual occultism, this major aspect of magical tradition has been ignored until fairly recently; now it is undergoing a considerable revival of attention. Contemporary concern with interrelationships, holism of life forms, and the environment, has helped to dispose of the rigid notion that all magical arts are essentially superstitious nonsense. No one will deny that there is much ignorance and superstition in the material purporting to be magical, handed down through the centuries. Ignorance and superstition abound in every aspect of human life - though often the superstition manifests as irrational prejudice and bigotry.

Practical magic is not limited to historical inheritance or slavish adherence to tradition. Each generation contributes certain organic changes to the overall structure of any spiritual or magical tradition, without necessarily moving away from or demolishing the tradition itself. This is because the magical arts are founded upon the collective sources of mythology and human consciousness in relationship to the land or planet. Nowadays we might say that magic is environmental. The changes in techniques and attitudes to magical arts are in part reflections of changes in society - though students of esoteric philosophy might suggest that changes in society are anticipated or even given impetus by changes in the magical arts. The concerns of magicians of one generation often manifest at large in the society of later generations - sometimes the manifestation is rapid, sometimes it is slow and subtle, permeating through long periods of historical time.

In our present context we should focus upon the use of images in the magical arts, upon the wide range of interrelated techniques in which the imagination is used in a relatively controlled manner, according to traditional patterns and techniques. The aim of this aspect of magic is to define certain key images and interact with them, to exchange and amplify energy through such interaction. This technique comes under the general heading of *visualisation* nowadays, and is widely used in various schools of meditation and therapy . As the magical arts inherit and still work with material from a variety of religious, mythic and cultural sources, we frequently use images of gods and goddesses for visualisation in magic.

Many people nowadays are familiar with visualisation of deities or mythic beings through the development of the theory of archetypes in Jungian, post-Jungian and transpersonal psychology. This helps, to a certain extent, in presenting magical art to a modern perception. While this therapeutic or modern psychological type of visualisation does indeed play a part in the magical arts, magical techniques and practices go a lot further.

One confused area of understanding for modern individuals, and indeed of practice in contemporary magical arts, is that of the reality or apparent reality of magical images such as goddess- or god-forms. This confusion is undoubtedly the result of modern materialist psychology, which has fastened upon mythic images, particularly in the case of Jungian and post-Jungian therapy and theory, and repeatedly asserted that they are mental and emotional constructs or inherent psychic forms with no entity, will, or reality, of their own.

Thus we frequently find modern magicians talking and even writing that one may 'use' a god-form to embody certain inherent psychic properties or energies, or to clarify one's own thinking through the psychological or psychotherapeutic effect of such images. Even the important word *archetype* (which has an ancient Greek origin) has been widely abused and misrepresented through the influence of modern psychology. Men now frequently consider the presence or power of a god, or the God, as a projection of an archetype, as some fragment of the male psyche. In some modern books on magic, this psychic fragment is said to benefit males by being projected or extruded as an imaginative form, filled with energy by various esoteric methods, and then deflated and reabsorbed. We might be tempted to observe the Freudian phallic undertones to this post-Jungian theory of magic!

Magic is often regarded solely as an art or science by which such projections are made. At a recent conference a trained psychologist asserted that her own practice of modern revival witchcraft consisted of projecting the *animus* and *anima* (as defined in Jungian theory) as, or into, the ancient God and Goddess forms, and that by doing so her group of fellow 'witches', male and female, were greatly balanced, healed, and liberated. This type of thinking is so far removed from actual magical practice through the ages, that we might wonder how it has crept into revival paganism at all - it certainly has no connection with genuine witchcraft.

In all the magical arts, as in pagan religion, the god- and goddess-forms are living entities, which act as vehicles or holistic aspects or harmonics of a universal God and Goddess, and are never regarded as projections of the human psyche. This might be flippantly considered as evidence of the ignorance of our ancestors, were it not for the fact that there is often a highly developed understanding of the human psyche in ancient religion, magic, metaphysics, and esoteric or magical practices. Indeed, complex and highly sophisticated discussions on this very subject permeated the philosophy and magical arts of the Classical world, and are known from even earlier sources such as Assyrian or Babylonian and Egyptian texts and fragments.

So our first assertion must be that the god (by which we mean any aspect of male-imaged divinity) in western magical arts is a real entity. This divine entity takes a number of forms defined by various streams of myth and religion. These forms or entities behave in quite distinct and characteristic ways when encountered in meditation, visualisation, or ritual working. Our second assertion is that these god-forms, variations of expression of a universal God (just as goddesses are variations of the universal Goddess), are not always subsumed under any one orthodox religious heading. While it would be accurate to say that many god-forms or images lead progressively towards a central figure, often defined as the Son of Light, and having centralising, harmonising solar powers, this god-form and related consciousness is not controlled or owned by any one orthodox religion. Furthermore, there are streams of consciousness and imagery, aspects of the God, which do not lead to this solar or central God-form. These can be of major importance in the arts of empowerment, and until recently have been given little attention in modern research publications and practice.

The question of polarity comes into all discussions and practices of this sort. The Light Son is often related in literature to a Dark Mother. But we seldom encounter any suggestion that we should work with a Dark Son and a Light Mother. Surely, this is the result of patriarchal political religion and monosexual propagandised images of divinity. Nor is it sufficient to rely upon a psychological interpretation, however valid this may be in a modern culture or nuclear family society context. Our ignorance of the absence of the Dark God is a terrible indictment upon our culture, just as much as our knowledge of the absence of the Dark Goddess.

An Essential Distinction

We need to be very clear at this point. We are not talking about images of 'evil' when we discuss dark god and goddess forms. There is a classic problem in this context found among modern meditators, visualisers and magicians, one which runs more deeply than personal psychological manifestations or life-problems. A typical scenario, rather comical if it were not so serious, is the one in which the would-be magician seeks to invoke the great God of the ancient world, known variously as Pan or Cernunnos (to whom we shall return shortly in more detail). Such invocations are always, without exception, successful, though the effect may vary from hidden and permeating results over a period of time, to a full sense of contact and presence and considerable power.

If anything like the second effect occurs, the poor religiously-conditioned, materialist-ridden magician often feels that he or she has conjured up something difficult, even evil, because of the level of raw power and the nature of the god himself. No sooner is the god present than he is hastily requested to depart! But the evil is in us, not in the god; if we were to pass through the *panic* and emerge on the other side, we would find that the god cleanses us of our corruptions, and that we no longer reflect our own fears and imbalances into exterior forms, be they humans or deities. In modern use, 'masters' have tended to replace the gods and heroes of the ancient world, performing similar functions but with an emphasis upon non-divinity (because of our historical monotheism).

The variety of male images and god-forms in western magic is large. How much of this variety derives from purely literary sources, and how much from practising magicians and living tradition, is very difficult to establish in a strict historical sense. As I hope to demonstrate in the examples and discussion below, a historical pinpointing of the sources of images is probably irrelevant to their authenticity or potential use in magical arts. More important is their general presence within an enduring tradition. This presence within the stream or flow of tradition is very important indeed, for it reveals the difference between a genuine god (or goddess) image, however masked or faint, and the product of modern fantasy or entertainment. God-forms do, of course appear in modern fantasy and entertainment, but not all images or characters that are said to be 'magical' are truly so.

Let us examine some of the basic sources for god-forms (always bearing in mind that these are also the basic sources for goddess-images).

The Tree of Life

Most images are definable upon the Tree of Life, a pan-cultural symbol which shows relationships between various traditional orders of existence, such as gods and goddesses, spirits, angels, and so forth, the human psyche and spirit, and the solar system. (See Figure 2). The Tree of Life is often described, in various publications, as deriving solely from Jewish mysticism and Kabbalah, but it has many western variants, plus, of course, further expressions worldwide. The form currently in use seems to be a fusion of neo-Platonic tradition with Renaissance Kabbalah and planetary and classical mythic patterns. It is a combination of classical Greek, Jewish, and western European lore such as that of Celtic bardic wisdom teachings and other poetic systems preserved in Europe for many centuries. Complex as all this sounds or reads on paper, the result is surprisingly simple and accessible.

My own theory, totally unproven, is that the Tree of Life is a pattern that reappears in each tradition, regardless of cultural or historical origins. It does so because of its inherent properties, by which our consciousness relates, even unwittingly, to the patterns of the solar system. Regardless of any such theories, it exists, and performs the remarkable task of linking and harmonising all inner or mythic patterns with those of the outer world, be it in the form of the human being or the solar system.

Origins and Mirroring of God-forms in Western Magic

God-forms, by which we can include for the moment images of archangels, angels and spiritual entities, though these are not true god-forms in their own right, come in a surprising number of guises. If we take an image such as an orthodox archangel found in both Jewish and Christian orthodox religions, we find this same entity in mystical practices and ritual magic. Whole in an orthodox sense, the archangel seems to be clearly defined, and in modern Christianity virtually defunct and ignored, in the magical arts the deeper resonance of the image often comes though. These deeper levels may contain old god-forms, which the orthodox religion has subsumed. Thus we cannot strictly call archangels, angels, heroes, saints, and so forth god-forms, but in certain circumstances and through alterations of consciousness, we may find god-forms attuned to them or awakening through their initial interface.

In the magical tradition such forms are derived from Classical, Middle Eastern, Celtic, and, less frequently nowadays, Norse or Scandinavian tradition. The Middle-Eastern variants are confined to those of Jewish religious origins, or of Christianity, though much of the Christianity in magical arts is inherited from Gnostic sources rather than Roman orthodoxy. There are some connections to ancient Egyptian religion, through the mirroring of god-forms within one another, but the majority of Egyptian symbolism in western magical arts was assembled no earlier than the nineteenth century. Exceptions to this are genuine Egyptian magical papyri which appeared in Europe from time to time, but these were of a late period and not necessarily connected to the ancient religion, more to Renaissance magic, Gnosticism, neo-Platonic tradition, and so forth.

The quality of *mirroring*, is important when we consider images and the forces within the images of gods and goddesses in meditation, magic, and spiritual traditions. Although I have used the term mirroring (thinking of the visual aspect of an infinity-box where mirrors are arranged to reflect one another), the concept is also one of holism, for there is no 'true original' of any god-form. We consider an image, usually defined by collective mythic tradition; within that image are older forms, variant forms, and, to the skilled visualiser or seer, future forms. They mirror one another to infinity, but for practical purposes we are usually aware of a specific set or a limited number of images.

This is where a true magician and an intellectual occultist or theoretician differ considerably. Both work with sets of images and patterns, but the theorist always tries to define originals into a rigid set. The working seer, shaman, or magician knows that images will change repeatedly, revealing inner aspects of themselves, yet always remain harmoniously true to the original starting image. Much confusion arises for students who cannot, initially grasp this, and who seek rigid, even dogmatic, forms, often at the expense of true magical experience. Men are particularly prone to this problem in western society, and tend to seek rigid authoritarian hierarchical god-forms and structures.

An example of the mirroring of god-forms will help to explain this process clearly. We can begin with the rather mysterious and virtually ignored English Saint George. He is a mythic saint, in other words he was not a historical martyr. Indeed, the Roman church removed him from the modern approved list of saints, as such mythic figures are generally set aside in the process of ossification within orthodox religions.

Saint George is really a magical image: the hero and the dragon, found in classical myth as Perseus. He links also to the Archangel Michael, often used as the model of (patriarchal) Light subduing darkness. But is this sufficient? If we look within these images, particularly that of St George, a remarkable sequence unfolds. It leads us away from a patriotic English Saint and dragon-slayer, towards a primal god of light and liberty, who does not kill the dragon or serpent of the earth, but is in truth empowered and set free by its transformative forces .

The earliest churches of St George, in Lydda, Palestine, are built upon ritual temple sites dedicated to Horus, the hawk god of Egypt. St George is sometimes shown with a hawk's head - symbol of pure dawn, flight into the eye of the sun. And, suddenly, this leads us westwards again, to an ancient youthful god of spring in Celtic tradition, the Hawk of May. This is only the merest summary of a series of connections supported by history, iconography, archaeology, and so forth. But in both psychological and magical terms, such mirrored gods are greatly empowering, while the rigid, firmly attributed images are always in danger of becoming stereotypes, or, more subtly, of imbuing stereotypes into the individual psyche.

A second example of a complex god-form, yet harmonically mirrored, is that of Merlin. People are surprised at the proposal that Merlin is a god rather than a magician, but it seems likely that historically the name 'Merlin' was a title assumed by certain prophets within a Welsh and Scottish line of tradition. This tradition linked back both to the Goddess of the Land, dating from at least as early as the megalithic culture of the West, and to her divine son or consort.

Today, of course, Merlin is seen as a stereotypical wise elder in modern fiction and popular belief, but we find that the earliest legends of Merlin show an entire life cycle, from prophetic youth, to mad wild-man of the woods, and only then to the elder. Merlin, particularly the young Merlin, is associated with the polarised power of two dragons within the earth (resonance of St George), with prophetic vision, and the knowledge of many worlds and orders of creation. He is similar in many ways to the young god Apollo in Greek tradition.[17]

So within the stereotypical elder Merlin is a harmonic set of reflections leading to a divinity, the primal Child of Light. As many of these connectives are shown in the pattern of the Tree of Life, let us now proceed to a summary of god-forms in western magic, referring to Figure 2.

God-forms Upon the Tree of Life

God-forms upon the Tree of Life are generally defined as follows, though there are a number of variants or alternatives, and no rigid or dogmatic formula.

10. Gods of the land, of nature, of Earth. May include heroes, ancestral beings, fairies and spirits of nature.

9. Lunar gods, ancestral deities, and certain older gods of water. May include heroes, and innerworld or otherworld male images that embody divine forces.

8. Mercury, the messenger god. Hermes, the Hermetic tradition.

7. Gods of the emotion and feeling: Orpheus, the Orphic tradition.

6. Apollo, solar deities. The Son or Child of Light. Gods of harmony, therapy, balance. The sacred kings and redeeming figures of world religion: Christ.

5. Mars: gods of taking, death, vigour, martial skills, and the transition between death and life. Gods of hunting, culling, herding and animals breeding appear here in one higher octave or form than that of the (10) earthly expressions.

4. Jupiter: the god of giving, creativity, outpouring energy, joy, mercy and compassion.

3. Saturn: the dark brooding gods, lords of endless time, mediators of grief and suffering, deep cosmic tides of change.

2. The Zodiac: deities or mythic images associated with the 12 signs of the pattern of heaven. Stellar deities in groups or holisms. Also identified with Neptune, not simply as a sea god (9) but as a great god of the ocean of stars. Functions of ferrying, wisdom, transition and enlightenment and awareness beyond death and beyond human personality are found here.

1. Ultimate Being, the primal God. Identified sometimes with Uranus, the father of all gods, and of course with the orthodox concept of God in formal religion.

10

EMPOWERMENT AND TRANSFORMATION: A DETAILED WORK PROGRAMME

Using Visualisation for Empowerment and Transformation

The Five Branches pattern may be utilised and activated in a variety of different ways. A basic training and self-initiation programme is possible, for either the individual or a small working group. In the ancient magical initiations of the Mysteries, the scenarios, patterns and archetypes, gods and goddesses, were ritually enacted as colourful and potent ceremonies. This may still be done today, providing we are realistic and allow for considerable changes of culture and consciousness, but as a basic modern method of working we may use regular, repeated visualisation.

Through active use of the imagination in work with each of the Branches, we cause a response, a resonance, of the energies within ourselves connected to each Branch. Furthermore, there is a broad correspondence between the Five Branches and the subtle energies and physical organs of the male body. There is no need to make detailed correlations or so-called definitive connections on this level, as the correspondence varies from person to person. Furthermore, the energy centres and their activation will vary during a lifetime, or even during the passage of a few hours of a day in some cases. This motion of the energy centres is seldom taken into account in rigid correspondences of chakras and subtle energies as published in most modern books. Some individuals, for example, need to liberate and enable movement of their energy centres, while others need quite the opposite and require a fixing and stabilising of their energies. The general pattern of the Five Branches of Warrior, Poet, Prophet Priest and King in relation to the male body, and subtle energies is shown in Figure 6.

Our suggested working timetable (see Figure 7) utilises the lunar cycle of energies, which effects both men and women strongly, as it does all life forms on the planet. This tidal cycle is more obviously known to women through the cycle of menstruation, but re-attuning to lunar cycles, or more accurately becoming properly aware of their presence within yourself, is an invaluable harmonising and transforming process for men.

With the methods described here we do not need to concern ourselves overmuch with the state of our subtle energies at commencement. Too much introspective or intellectual concern over whether one's energies are fixed, fluid, rigid, or loose, is usually a distraction or even an evasion of the true work within one's self. The patterns and sequences of imaginative encounters in the exercises which follow will, of their own accord, act in a balancing and transformative way upon each of the Five Branches within ourselves, thus balancing and empowering the associated energies of the organism.

It is inevitable in any discussion of inner forces that the boundaries between images or seeming entities or archetypes, and the energies that they embody become blurred. As a general rule the method works simply by regarding the beings, entities or archetypes as real, and not as symbols or explanations of energies within oneself. The key to this circular debate or riddle is to consider your own entity - are you a being, an image, or energy? The answer to all of these questions is yes.

The Three Thresholds

Development through visualisation in the Male Mysteries can be defined in several stages, with an overall threefold pattern. The three main stages are termed the *Three Thresholds,* to give a clear definition of their function. They also resonate with the triplicity of the Three Faces of the God in myth and legend, and with the Three Mothers. Within each of the Three Thresholds, is another threefold pattern, three lesser thresholds or stages of development, giving a total of nine in all. We shall work through each of these stages, crossing each threshold, small and great, through direct visualisation. The method is actually much simpler to undertake and experience than it sounds when described in a summary of this sort, as each of the lesser and greater thresholds merge harmonically with one another.

We will consider (in Chapter11) how these might be practically enacted by a small group of men taking each of the roles in turn. It must be emphasised that the basic familiarity and practice of the imaginative and visualising aspects of the method should be well established before working through the group enactment method. Without the basic visualisation and familiarity with the symbols, imaginative beings, and energies involved, the psycho-dramatic or ritual method cannot be fully developed by an independent group. Please note that the emphasis here is that there is no 'authority' or 'guru' in such a group. The King is in ourselves, the Worker or primal Man ennobled, and is not a human authority figure.

The Room with Four Doors

We will be working within a well established visualising and meditational scenario, which involves imagining a room and then entering it. Such scenarios have been used for thousands of years in the spiritual, magical, mystical or primal initiatory arts, and carry within them considerable power. Through gentle repetition of such exercises we are able to attune to them, and benefit from them. There is no suggestion here of remarkable will-power or intense concentration - while basic concentration is indeed necessary for visualising, excessive effort will actually slow your development. The powers of the imagination tend to develop through relaxed repetition rather than a mental equivalent of muscle-building.

Visualising the Room

The work begins by relaxing, eyes closed, breathing steadily, and calming your mind. *(The exercise of Silence, Appendix 1, is recommended for this purpose.)* The next stage is to build an image of a room. *(The shape of this room is shown in Figure 8 and should be carefully studied and remembered, as you will build this shape into a series of visualisations.)*

It is a very plain room with five walls. You sit at one end of the room, building its image around you. To your right and left are two walls which angle together to meet behind you. Before you are two further right and left hand walls, sloping in towards the fifth smallest wall at the far end of the room. This fifth wall is a mirror, and in it you see a reflection of the four angled walls of the room, with yourself sitting in the furthest corner where the walls meet. On each of the four walls to your right and left is a door.

You enter into this image, feeling a sense of calm expectation. After a short period, you gently dissolve the image of the room, open your eyes, and return to your surroundings.

Notes

1. This deceptively simple visualisation is the foundation for the

Figure 7 - The Twelve Week Cycle

This twelve-fold cycle is recommended as the basic pattern for a work programme of meditation and visualisation in the Male Mysteries. It may also be used, like our other figures, as a guideline for cycles of movement or sacred dance combined with visualisation.

The cycle turns for twelve weeks if a lunar pattern is followed, and this is particularly helpful for modern men who have lost contact with their inherent relationship to natural rhythms. There is a popular delusion that males are 'solar' and females 'lunar' in rhythm, partly due to patriarchal propaganda and ignorance. Both men and women are affected by lunar and solar cycles, and our powers of imagination linked to sexual energies and life forces are enhanced by attuning consciously to a lunar cycle.

As a solar cycle, the twelve-fold rhythm will take one year, or twelve hours of twelve consecutive days. For practical work, the lunar cycle is recommended first before working to the longer or shorter time-scales.

The Cycle of Encounters with Companions, Goddesses, and Gods

TIME: *Week One* *Week Two* *Week Three* *Week Four*

| | | | | |

MOON: *Dark* *Waxing* *Full* *Waning* *Dark*

(Begin the second phase in Week Five, third phase in Week Nine.)

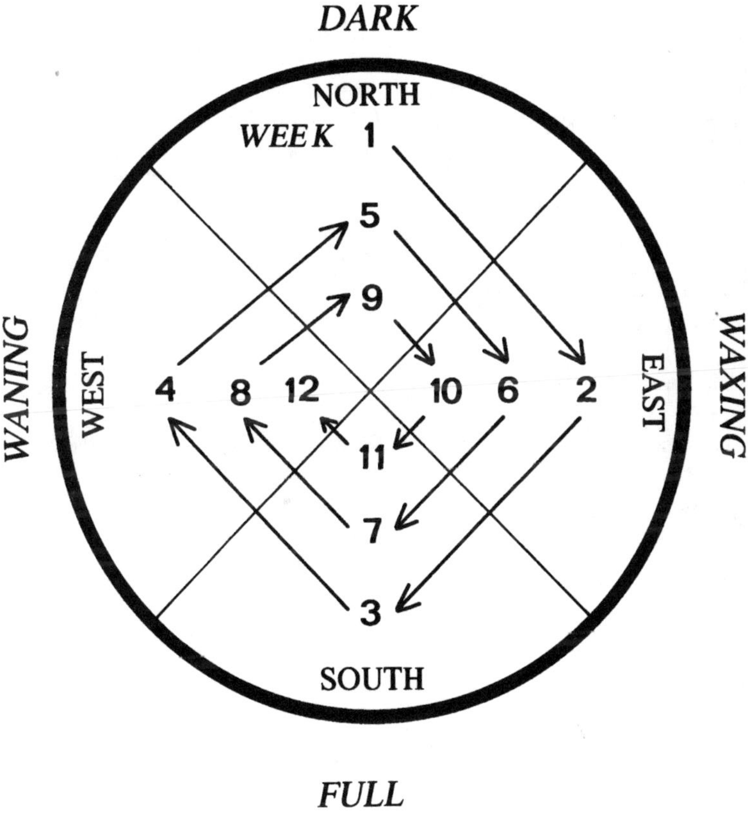
DARK
NORTH
WEEK 1
5
9
WANING
WEST
4
8
12
10
6
2
EAST
WAXING
11
7
3
SOUTH
FULL

Figure 8 - The Room with Four Doors

The Room is a form of Sacred Space, a defined location in which energies and consciousness work. We see classic examples of this in temples and worship sites, ranging from prehistoric to modern. These physical forms of Sacred Space, be they stone circles or cathedrals, attune energies of many kinds, harmonising geomantic or natural forces with those of humanity.

In visualisation, the model of a room is particularly powerful, with differing effects depending upon its shape. The visualised space may be located within a physical space which is a room of any suitable shape, or entirely within a regular rhythm of imaginative work upon inner levels.

Five is the number of man (see Figures 5 and 6), hence the use of a pentagonal room. This is located within an implicit hexagonal shape (see Figure 4), which is in turn within the Fourfold Circle (see Figure 1). The Four Companions - Warrior, Poet, Prophet and Priest - are encountered through Four Doors (see Chapter 10). Three thresholds or octaves of transformation and encounter are possible through using the Room as a model for shaping consciousness and energy: The Companions, The Goddesses, The Gods.

1 = Warrior
2 = Poet
3 = Prophet
4 = Priest
5 = King

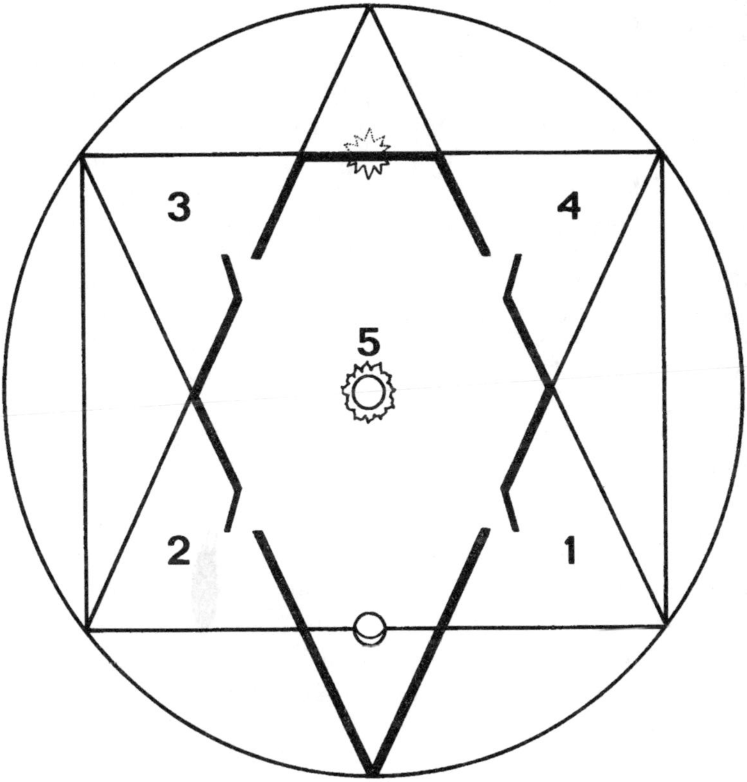
3
4
5
2
1

entire pattern of initiation through the Five Branches. It should be repeated several times, without strain or determination, until the feeling of the room and of being within it is established. Do not rush into the later stages of the visualisations until this basic image of the room is established and you can pass in and out of it without great difficulty. 'Without great difficulty' means that you should be able to imagine being in the room and to hold that image and feeling for a few minutes. There is no requirement that it becomes an alternative reality or that the image must be absolutely firm for long periods of time. You will find that the duration of the visualisation and the alternative reality of the room build naturally, particularly when you work in the later stages where the room is peopled.

2. The Doors and Mirror. It is often found while working with this type of empowered image, that you are attracted to certain doors or to study yourself in the mirror. As a general rule, you should calmly relax out of such initial attractions. You may find the reverse, of course, for some people find the doors threatening or difficult to visualise. It is also quite common to fail to see yourself in the mirror, or to see a distorted image. As discussed in our earlier chapters, the Mysteries do not use free association or similar techniques found in modern psychology. It is the actual *shape* of the room, and in the latter stages, its occupants, that are important in this type of work, not free associative reactions, attractions or subjective impressions.

Simplicity is always the key to this initial stage of the work. By breathing steadily and relaxing it is possible to establish the basic image of the room, doors, and mirror, without entering into any activity or distraction. Building the room, dissolving it, rebuilding it...dissolving it. That is all that is required at this stage.

3. Breathing and Imaging. You may find it helpful to breath steadily in and out (no breath holding or unusual breathing exercises or postures are necessary for this) and count breaths. A typical pattern might be to count ten steady breaths in and out while building the image of the room, two breaths for each wall, for example. Then a dissolving of the image for the space of three breaths in and out. This method may help if you have difficulty in initially building the image, but it must not become obsessive or any type of rigid method, as that would undermine the work in hand. Eventually your breathing becomes unconscious again in the later stages of the visualisations, so dependence upon counting breaths is merely a trick or interim stage.

Encountering the Five Branches

The Warrior

First we build the image of the Room with Four Doors. We find ourselves in the room, with its mirror on the far wall, and four plain doors, each one being closed. We look at the floor of the room, and see there three symbols inlaid in metal into the floor. *(See Figure 9 for these inlaid symbols.)* The first one is of silver, in the pattern of the full and crescent Moon, and is nearest to us. The second one is of gold, in the shape of the flaming Sun; this is in the centre of the room. The third symbol merges into the base of the mirror - we see half of it, a radiating star of varied colours, while the other half is reflected in the mirror to complete the image. We pause and consider these three symbols, meditating upon them for a few moments.

Now we stand upright, and taking three paces forward, find that our feet rest upon the first emblem. As we touch it we hear a door opening behind us to the right. Looking in the mirror ahead, we see that a Warrior has emerged from that door, and he stands just behind our right shoulder. We look upon him in the mirror, and know that he has come firstly to protect us during our training, but more important to share his skill and knowledge with us, so that we will develop as warriors ourselves.

We pause in silence, feeling the presence of the warrior as he stands at our right shoulder. *(Here a pause is made for communion. This is judged separately on each occasion.)*

Now the Warrior turns and passes through his door. As the door closes, we step back from the Moon mark, and return to the end of the room. Now we slowly dissolve the image of the room, and emerge to our regular surroundings.

Notes

1. The usual method in this type of work is to see the innerworld contacts or archetypes in the mirror, without turning around. This technique greatly assists the appearance of the innerworld beings. The type of Warrior is not predefined in this visualisation (nor are the images of the other Branches), as the Warrior that appears in the mirror will be of the type most suited to your own needs and work.

2. The Presence of the Inner Warrior. The length of this sense of presence is left entirely to your own judgement, though it is usually fairly short to start with. It is not unusual during this silent phase for the sense of actual presence to greatly intensify, and for a flow of

Figure 9 - The Three Emblems

Working within Sacred Space, the Pentagonal Room has three Thresholds, each defined by a point of location within the space. By moving physically and in visualisation, we enable our crossing of these thresholds, and our encounters with the Companions, Goddesses and Gods, of the Male Mysteries. We begin at the entrance and exit point of the room, where all energies manifest as the physical body; all Companions, Goddesses and Gods manifest through the physical body.

The first threshold is broadly defined as Lunar consciousness, and this is where we begin when we enter into meditation and visualisation for the first time, or upon the first level of altered awareness. This involves encounters with the Poet and Warrior, the right and left hand energies and entities of male mental and emotional being. The Poet and Warrior enable us to proceed to the centre of the room, the second threshold, or Solar consciousness.

The second threshold of altered awareness is where we meet the Prophet and Priest, the right and left hand entities of male spiritual and transpersonal being. They enable us to proceed to the third threshold, broadly defined as Stellar consciousness. At the second threshold of Solar consciousness, we are in the centre of the Sacred Space, balanced by all four Companions. This is the first point or centre of Kingship. Two further central points are found, through crossing the consciousness and energy thresholds of the four Goddesses and then of the four Gods (see Chapter 10).

The Threshold of Stellar consciousness marks the transition or mirror between one level of the room and the next.

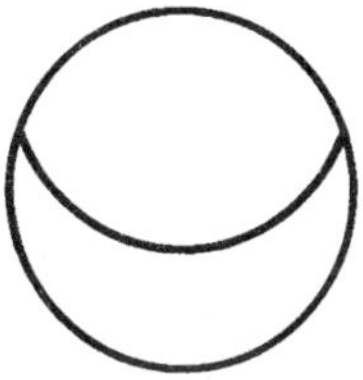

wordless communication and energy to occur. The innerworld Warrior empowers our physical energies and skills, our will, our endurance. He will also teach or enable development of the senses through special training techniques, and will often communicate matters concerned with our physical health and fitness. The Warrior also instils a sense of honour, charity and tempering of power to favour and assist others, even at the expense of one's self-interest.

3. The Departure. You may find that the Warrior departs of his own accord, or alternatively you should slowly withdraw from the sense of communication when you are ready. Some men will find that it is easier to withdraw from the room while the Warrior remains within it. On leaving the room, you should make notes briefly describing your experience. In many cases, the innerworld contact gives you something. If this occurs note what it is and draw it if it is unusual (which is often the case). Such gifts are later used as meditative tools or emblems in their own right, encapsulating the entire experience into one powerful key image. These are a type of magical implement, and may have physical counterparts.

Encountering the Poet

First we build the image of the Room with Four Doors, and finding ourselves within this room, take three paces forward to the first emblem upon the floor, inlaid as a silver full and crescent Moon. As our feet touch the mark, we hear a door open behind us to our left. Looking in the mirror on the far wall, we see a Poet (or Bard) enter the room, behind our left shoulder. Looking upon him, we realise that he has come to give us inspiration, and that he will share his skill and knowledge with us, so that our own power of poetry, memory, and feeling will develop within.

We pause in silence, feeling the presence of the Poet as he stands at our left shoulder. *(A pause for silent communion here.)* Now the Poet turns and passes through his door. As the door closes we step back from the Moon mark, and return to the end of the room. Now we slowly dissolve the image of the room, and emerge to our regular surroundings.

Notes

1. The presence of the Poet or Bard empowers our inspirations, feelings, and sensitivity. Innerworld poets, however, are not wilting sensitive types; if they appear as true Poets or Bards, they are men of considerable power, acting as storehouses and teachers of vast collections of wisdom, music, song, poetry and magical traditions.

2. While the magic of the Warrior is that of developing disciplines of both strength and flexibility of mind and body, the magic of the Poet is that of developing the arts of inspiration, memory, and the feelings. Each Branch has its own stream or teaching of magic, in which accessible outer skills merge imperceptibly into unusual abilities and raising of the level of consciousness and power.

The Second Threshold

Encountering the Prophet

We begin by entering the Room with Four Doors. When we are within the room, in our inner vision, we step up to the first mark, the emblem of the Moon in the floor. As we do so, two doors open behind us, and in the Mirror ahead we see our Warrior and Poet come into the room, and stand on either side, just behind us.

We now intend to step into the centre of the room, to the emblem of the Sun set in gold in the floor. As we take the first step, the Mirror on the far wall clouds over until we cannot see the Warrior and Poet, nor can we see ourselves. Suddenly a nameless fear enters us, and takes form as personal doubts, worries and insecurities. Just as we are about to step back, we feel a firm hand on our right shoulder. The Warrior whispers a word in our ear (......). As he does so we find that we are filled with the power of the Warrior, and we know that it is our own Power. We feel another hand upon our left shoulder, and the Poet whispers a word in our ear (......). As he does so we are filled with the knowledge, perception, and feeling of the Poet, and it is our own knowledge, perception, and feeling.

The Mirror clears, and we take three firm paces forward to stand upon the central emblem. The Warrior and Poet step back, and for a moment we stand alone, waiting ready. *(Pause for silent meditation here.)*

Immediately to our left is a door. It slowly opens, and a Prophet enters the room to stand before us, on our left hand side. In the mirror we see reflections of the Warrior and Poet, and ourselves, but the Prophet we see directly before us. He looks into our eyes and a silent communication passes between him and us. *(Silent communion here.)*

(Repeat exit sequence as before.)

Encountering the Priest

We beginby entering the Room with Four Doors. When we are within the room, in our inner vision, we step up to the first mark, the emblem of the Moon in the floor. As we do so, two doors open behind us, and in the Mirror ahead we see our Warrior and Poet come into the room and stand on either side, just behind us.

We now intend to step into the centre of the room, to the embelm of the Sun set in gold on the floor. As we take the first step, the Mirror on the far wall clouds over until we cannot see the Warrior and Poet, nor can we see ourselves. Suddenly a nameless fear enters us, and takes form as personal doubts, worries, insecurities. Just as we are about to step back, we feel a firm hand on our right shoulder. The Warrior whispers a word in our ear (.....) and as he does so we find that we are filled with the power of the Warrior, and we know that it is our own Power. We feel another hand upon our left shoulder, and the Poet whispers a word in our ear (.....) as he does so we are filled with the knowledge, perceptionand feeling of the Poet, and it is our won knowledge, perception and feeling.

The Mirror clears and we take three firm paces forward to stand upon the central emblem. The Warrior and Poet step back and for a moment we stand alone, waiting ready. *(Pause for silent meditation here.)*

Immediately to our right is a door. It slowly opens and a Priest enters the room to stand before us on our right hand side. In the mirror we see reflections of the Warrior and Poet, and ourselves, but the Priest we see directly before us. He looks into our eyes, and a silent communication passes between him and us. *(Silent communication here.)*

(Repeat exit sequence as before.)

Notes

On returning to outer consciousness, the usual notes are taken. There should be a pause of one day after the encounter of the Prophet and Priest. (See Figure 7 for potential time scales of working with these exercises.)

What Should They Look Like?

In this series of visualisations members of the actual Branches are not described in detail, as they will appear differently for each individual. Nor is there any requirement that your Warrior, Poet, Priest, and Prophet be of the same time period, culture or type. There seems to be a general rule with this type of imaginative inner work that the contacts appear in the form of people from the ancestral past. A further general but not inflexible rule is that they are from cultures that relate in some way to your own, either ancestrally or in terms of general tradition and consciousness.

Although the general rule and experience is that the inner contacts or people seem to be from the ancestral past or from past idealised societies or places, there is no reason why they should not be from other worlds altogether or even from, the future. Having said this, I would stress very strongly that caution is needed in this respect as the entire experience must never be allowed to degenerate into whimsy or fantasy. Images from popular entertainment such as films, television, science fiction and so forth are emphatically not in the mainstream of the Mysteries, and can even be misleading and weakening under obsessive or flippant circumstances.

The general rule is that the contacts are from the ancestral or cultural past, because there is a connection between the deeper more potent levels of consciousness and energy and the apparent flow of historical time. The deeper we go within ourselves, the more we seem to link to past humanity and to other life forms. Hence future contacts are extremely rare, while contact with beings from other worlds altogether are less rare but are often difficult to cope with or are potentially confusing. The value of spiritual or consciousness-changing traditions is that they give enormous flexibility within certain simple and known parameters. If we stay within these parameters the changes are certain to occur.

For Westerners this broadly ancestral or cultural steam of contact can produce a surprisingly wide range of innerworld people including those from virtually unknown past civilisations, simple ancestral societies, and in some cases contacts that appear to be definable in terms of more recent modern history. Eastern societies still have a vast range of mythic entities well defined in tradition and religion, and so eastern inner contacts tend to work through such well known forms.

Those of us who are Black, Asian, or Oriental, but within the Western civilisation, are able to draw upon a mixed range of inner contacts and will eventually need to settle into an ancestral or specific stream of energy that satisfies both intellectual and intuitive needs. This can only come though experience in meditation and visualisation, hence the need for all types of people within the Mysteries regardless of their roots, to have open visualisations and flexible techniques that are not attuned to rigid teachings, dogmas, predetermined images or limited innerworld or religious beings.

While working through these exercises it would be harmonious to find that each of the Five Branches was say a persona from ancient Greece or that they epitomised the Four Directions or noble castes of Celtic primal civilisation. In practice this seldom happens so do not be too surprised if your Poet and Warrior, Prophet and

Priest, are from seemingly different times and cultures. In most working patterns, the innerworld contacts remain constant, but there are occasional instances where the contact will spontaneously change appearance or personality during the higher levels of empowered working. If such a change occurs it needs to be carefully assessed, and if necessary the next visualisation can be addressed to one's original contact or to the new one. If you seek your first contact, and he is always replaced by the further contact or persona, then this second form is the new archetype or innerworld contact for your new level of consciousness and energy.

In normal work a major change of consciousness and energy is embodied by the change from working with the representative of a specified Branch (Warrior, Poet, etc.) through to working with the god or goddess behind that Branch. This change or octave transformation is steered to a certain extent by the structure of the visualisations and the working pattern defined in our set of exercises.

The Sleeping King: Awakening, Healing and Crowning

The Cycle of Visualisations and Encounters

Our basic working pattern is founded upon a twelve week cycle, divided into three lunar months. The lunar synchronisation is not essential but is easy to follow, and will enhance the subtle energies that arise within such regular visualisations and transformative exercises.

The Three Cycles are:

1. Encountering the Branches.
2. Encountering the Goddesses.
3. Encountering the Gods.

The twelve-week pattern involves the Three Thresholds each of which has a holism or minor cycle or rhythm within it. This cyclic rhythmic work is very beneficial, particularly when linked to the natural lunar cycle, as it re-establishes basic energy patterns within us, those from which men in particular have become separated to their loss.

Within each cycle the separate parts are, in themselves, simple visualisations which lead towards the culmination and completion of the cycle.

There is no requirement, however, that you force your way through all three major cycles if you are averse to doing so. The first cycle, encountering the Branches of Warrior, Poet, Prophet, and Priest may be repeated as often as you wish before moving on to the second one. The cycle of encountering the goddesses, however, should come before attempting the cycle of encountering the gods, as this is how men achieve maturity and balance with the more powerful forces of the Mysteries.

The first cycle will, of its own accord, go a long way towards awakening our energies. There is an important correlation between the three cycles, and the major myth of the sleeping and wounded King found in many forms worldwide, and directly relevant to the Male Mysteries.

The Sleeping and Wounded King

In various legends, we find the theme of the sleeping and wounded King. The basic story is that a King has been wounded deeply, and is in a coma or sleep somewhere between life and death.[18]

Many powerful myths and rituals revolve around finding and awakening the sleeping King, and making him whole. Even orthodox Christianity is firmly based upon a death and resurrection myth. In Arthurian legend, for an example with both Christian and pagan Celtic roots , the wounded Arthur is carried away over the sea to a magical island, where the goddess of healing and rebirth will restore him to life at the time of greatest need for his people.

This myth has an analogy in all humans, male or female, but we are concerned here with its specific relevance to the Male Mysteries. The man entering the Mysteries is both primal worker and sleeping wounded King. The King has to be awakened, healed, and finally crowned. These three stages of transformation correspond to the three cycles of the Mystery as follows:

1. Awakening the sleeping King: Encountering the Four Branches.
2. Healing his wounds: Encountering the Four Goddesses.
3. Crowning in full realisation: Encountering the Four Gods.

In each cycle the Fifth Branch, King or Worker, is always our selves. The same cycle would work in a Womens' Mystery as follows:

1. Encountering the Four Companion or Sister Branches of Womanhood.
2. Encountering the Gods.
3. Encountering the Goddesses.

A 12 Week Working Timetable

This variable timetable should be regarded only as a general guide, and not as a rigid schedule. The order of development is important, and should not be jumped through or altered, but the timescale for each Branch and for the later deeper encounters will vary according to the individual or group. The best procedure would be to adopt the short time-scale suggested here initially, but to expand or contract any longer time-cycles according to need, intuition, and growing experiences. The Mysteries, or any inner training, be it magical or spiritual or a combination of both, are not hobbies or temporary interests. Knowing yourself is the task of a lifetime. Changing yourself, however, is an ever present potential.

Short Time-scale

1. *Building the Room with Four Doors*
This exercise should be done daily; once per day is enough, but twice would be more effective. The visualisation should be done at the same time and if possible in the same location every day. This is an individual training exercise, regardless of any group work. When the building of the room has become reasonably effective, you should proceed to the next stage of the work.

2. *The People in the Room*
The first encounters are undertaken singly: the Warrior first, then the Poet. This order may be reversed if necessary, though the order of the next encounters, those of Prophet and Priest would normally remain. A basic short time-table would be as follows:

Day 1: The Warrior (duration variable).
Day 2: The Poet (duration variable).
Day 3: Pause (day 3, rest from visualisation. Note any dreams or intimations that seem to be connected to the workings. Do not push or rush into the next stage without this break).
Day 4: The Prophet (duration variable).
Day 5: The Priest (duration variable).
Day 6: Pause (as in Day 3 above).
Day 7: Begin cycle again with visualisation of empty room, then proceed from Day 1 to Day 6.

The cycle of encountering the Warrior/Poet/Prophet/Priest takes one week. It should be worked through as an ideal cycle of three times, thus taking three weeks, with approximately 30 minutes per day. You would then break and rest from visualising for the fourth week of the month.

Lunar Timing

Ideally this cycle should match the lunar cycle, which has a regular effect upon the life energies of all entities. To fit the working in this manner, simply calculate backwards from the dark of the Moon, letting that be at the end of the fourth week, the resting week. This means that the full Moon will be approximately at the end of the second cycle or week of encounters. See Figure 7.

The Four Goddesses

You enter the Room with Four Doors, and immediately the Poet and Warrior enter and join you. Together you step towards the centre of the chamber, and stand upon the second emblem, the image of the Sun set in gold into the floor. The Warrior and Poet stand behind you to the right and left. As you step onto the emblem, the Prophet and Priest emerge from the two doors in front of you, and stand before you. You are now in the centre of the room, in the centre of a square, marked at each corner by Four Companions, the Warrior, the Poet, the Prophet and the Priest. It is time to step forward three paces to the third and last emblem, embedded into the mirror-wall ahead, half in the room, half reflected in the mirror.

You formulate your will to step forward, and feel a nameless and formless fear, a degree of pure panic, causing your hair to rise and your skin to crawl. You feel a presence in the chamber standing directly before you, and recognise this as the presence of the Guardian of all Thresholds. He forbids you to step further.

Now the Prophet and the Priest step closer, and the Prophet places one hand upon the small of your back. The Priest places one hand upon the top of your head, and you feel a flow of energy like fire run up your spine. The Poet and Warrior each take your elbows in a firm grip, and as all four support you you feel a sense of weightlessness and ecstasy. *(Pause here for short meditation.)*

Suddenly the Four Companions throw you forward into the mirror: the shock of this movement dispels the sense of panic, and you pass right through the mirror into the reflected room beyond. *(Brief pause here.)*

Encountering the First Goddess

This room is empty, and is the mirror image of the one that you have left. There are four walls with doors in them, tapering to a narrow point at the far end of the room. You know that to return to your outer consciousness, you must cross this room, and leave from the far side. There are no emblems in the floor of the room, and it is silent, waiting. *(Pause here.)*

You feel awake, alert, ready, yet uncertain of what will happen in this empty room. Cautiously you take a step forward into the chamber, until the first pair of doors are on your right and left. As you do so, the door on your right opens, and a Warrior Goddess emerges from it.

The Warrior Goddess is tall and vigorous, she carries a sharp-pointed spear. A portion of her long red hair is brushed up and fixed into a tall crest, while the rest flows down her back like the mane of a horse. Her face is beautiful and savage and she looks directly into your eyes, challenging you to reveal your skill and potential. As she looks at you you feel the inner fire aroused by the touch of the Priest and Prophet burning within your blood and rising to your head. As it rises the Warrior Goddess lifts her spear above her head in a sign of victory. Then she begins to weave a circle dance around you, making many turns and twists. As she does so you feel her awareness within your own, and stand in stillness, communing with her power. *(Silent contemplation here.)*

Now the Warrior Goddess pauses in her dance, and stands directly before you, looking down at you. She holds a token or gift in one hand, and gives this to you. She steps aside and motions that you must walk to the far end of the room. As you do so you see a familiar chair in that far corner, and as you turn to sit upon it you realise that the goddess has vanished. You sit, and look at the pattern of the room, with the mirror on the far wall. Now you quietly dissolve the room, and return to your outer awareness.

Encountering the Second Goddess

(At this stage the individual may choose how to proceed. He may work directly with the reversed or second room, by building the room as it appears after passing through the mirror. Alternatively he may use the visualisation in which the Four Companions pass him through the mirror into the empty room. If in doubt, or if you try the more direct method and it does not seem to work fully, repeat the visualisation of passing through the mirror.)

Upon entering and standing in the second room, you hear a door open to your left. You turn to look in that direction, and see a Goddess of Inspiration and Intuition.

She holds a tiny flame in her cupped hands, and she seems to flow and change colour as you look upon her. She looks into your eyes and the flame in her hands suddenly flashes and rises up; as it does so you feel the inner fire rising up your spine. *(Pause here.)* Slowly she begins to circle around you, and as she moves you feel a flow of ideas, concepts, intuitions, attuning to your own awareness. As her movement increases in speed, her changing colours seem to flow into a pattern of light, and you pause to contemplate her presence. *(Silent pause here.)*

Now the Goddess of Inspiration and Intuition stands before you, and gives you a token or gift. She indicates that you should move to the far end of the room, where you see a familiar chair. As you turn to sit in this chair, you hear a door closing. Now you are alone in a familiar room, and slowly you return to outer consciousness.

Encountering the Third Goddess

You enter the Second Room, and take six paces forward to stand in the centre. The room is very empty and still, the four doors remain closed. As you stand in silent meditation in the centre of the still room, you feel a slight movement beneath your feet, as if the ground is trembling. Gradually you become aware of an energy arising from beneath, up out of the ground below, through the floor, and into your body. This is the power of the Goddess of the Land.

As the power rises through your body, it reaches your genitals, and triggers a powerful sexual desire. As you feel this desire, the door on your left opens and an aged and hideous woman enters the room. She slowly raises her left hand and your intense sexual desire increases until the energy begins to rise upwards towards your heart.

The Goddess of the Land fills you with both desire and aversion, longing, fear, and deep respect. You do not know what to do. She steps close to you and looks in your eyes. A wordless communion passes between you. *(Silent pause here.)*

Now images of the primal land emerge in your vision, the pure timeless land, uncorrupted, unabused, and you know that you will give your life to restore that land if the Goddess asks you to do so.

She lays her withered hand upon your throat, and you feel the intense sexual desire rise like a breath of wind to impel your voice to speak. You utter the words that come freely... *(Spontaneous words uttered here.)*

As you speak you see the crone change into a young woman of calm appearance and great beauty; she smiles upon you and the sexual desire gently harmonises into a feeling of peace and fulfilment. The Goddess of the Land indicates a chair at the far end of the room, and you walk towards it. As you turn to sit, you hear a door closing behind you. Now you return to outer consciousness.

Encountering the Fourth Goddess

You enter the room, and as you do so the two doors to your right and left open simultaneously. The Warrior Goddess and the Inspiration Goddess enter the room and stand to your right and left, holding your elbows in a tight grip. They walk with you to the centre of the room, and the third door on your left opens, and the aged crone enters the chamber. She stands directly in front of you, challenging you to proceed no further, for to take another step is to die. You speak the words that you uttered spontaneously when you first met her, and as you do so a great stillness descends upon the room. *(Silent pause here.)*

From deep beneath the floor, seeming to come from within the heart of the earth itself, a slow resonant drum beat sounds. The three goddesses step away from you and begin to move slowly with this beat, circling around you in a grave and stately weaving dance. With each step their shape and age and colour changes. Gradually the speed increases, and the drumming sounds intensifies. The three figures now whirl and spin about in a blur of colour, a host of changing faces. Within these faces you see momentarily your own mother, your sisters, your lovers, and many more familiar beloved yet unknown to you.

The beating drum rises to a rapid continuous throbbing sounds, and suddenly stops. The shape-changing host of women rushes in upon you, and resolves into three goddess, the Goddess of the Land, the Goddess of Inspiration, and the Goddess of Warriors. Each one carries in her hand a different coloured sword, and for an instant it seems that they will cut off your head. You stand still, awaiting whatever will come. *(Silent pause here.)*

The three goddesses have disappeared, and the fourth door stands open. Through it you see the depth of space filled with swirling stars. In the centre of that vastness is a slowly spiralling cloud of silver grey and white, shot through with many flashes of colour. A figure, wrapped in a dark robe with a deep hood pulled over her face slowly approaches you from within that spiral of stars. As she draws closer your vision of her seems to cloud over, yet the sense of presence grows. Now her presence fills the room yet she cannot be seen. You attend upon her in silent communion, for she is the Great Goddess of all being. *(Silent contemplation.)*

Gradually you become aware of a quiet empty room, and yourself standing in the centre of that room. Before you is a familiar chair, and you walk to this and sit. Now you return to outer awareness, leaving the second room behind.

The Four Gods

Before we move onto the visualisations for the four gods, a brief introduction to their nature and power should be given. Although we can find historical mythic content in the images used, and partly relate the god-forms to specific deities from the pantheons of various cultures, these are not cultural or historically defined gods. They are, in one sense, the gods behind the gods, and they are also the gods within each and every man. No man can come to the gods within until he has truly encountered the power of the Goddess.

In formal religion gods and goddesses always tend towards an increasingly defined presentation; as a society develops and becomes more civilised or complex, so do the gods and goddesses rigidify and become less fluid. In the Mysteries, however, the deeper aspects of deity were explored, the most important concept being that any god or goddess has a multifold nature. In our modern restoration of the Male Mysteries the main god-forms, archetypes and images inherent within human consciousness and history are resolved into four gods. These in turn are unified into one Being. By working through this archetypical and magical pattern, a man comes to inner kingship.

While much of this seems complex when described, the actual experience, given form by guided visualisation, or in ritual pattern making, replaces thousands of words and pointless analysis. Nevertheless, a short summary of the attributes of each of the four gods is helpful before we enter into the actual visualisations and contact their power directly. If you have worked through the encounters with the Four Companions and the Four Goddesses, the effect of what follows in this chapter will be very powerful indeed.

The Nature of the Four Gods

Just as we encountered the Branches of Warrior, Poet, Prophet, and Priest as Companions, then as Goddesses, so do we encounter them as gods. A god is a male-defined image for polarised universal power. But a god is not an analogy or a substitute, he is also a living entity, just as you and I are living entities. Never make the mistake of thinking that you are dealing with 'symbolism' in this work - symbols are used to weave the fabric of the visualisation, but the entities that populate it are real; possibly more real than ourselves as their existence is not limited by serial time or corporeal cycles of birth and death. Let us briefly consider each of the four gods:

1. The Warrior God: a god of compassion and severity.
2. The Poet God: a god of love and death.
3. The Prophet God: a god of reason and madness.
4. The Priest God: a god of light and darkness.

All four gods merge in the central unity of the Divine Son, or in man as the sacred priest-king who mediates their forces to the land and to all living beings. The perfect goal of humanity is to mediate the awareness of all Being to all Being, and specifically to all beings in our own world, the planet Earth.

To give some examples of cultural god-forms relating to four gods of the Branches, we would need to find at least two culturally defined deities for each of the four primal gods of the Mystery.

1. The Warriors' god of compassion and severity (life-giving/life taking) finds cultural expression in deities such as Jupiter and Mars.[19]

2. The Poets' god of love and death finds cultural expression in deities such as Orpheus, or in Celtic tradition Oenghus.[20]

3. The Prophets' god of madness and reason finds cultural expression in deities such as Pan, Apollo, or in Celtic tradition Cernunnos and Mabon.[21]

4. The Priests' god of light and darkness finds cultural expression in deities such as Christ and the great Saviour figures of world religion. Note that the light and darkness are not antagonistic but unified, each unable to Be without the other. Polarity out of Unity, Unity in Polarity.

In this last Branch, we find the Order of Sacred or Divine Kingship, defined in the Christian Mystery as the Order of Melchizadek, but by no means limited to that variant.

As a general rule, the detailed appearance of the gods and goddesses has been left to your own inspiration and vision, though they are firmly within world traditions for such inner work. In some schools of inner development, both psychological and spiritual or magical, long and detailed descriptions of archetypes, gods and goddess, or visualisation scenarios are used extensively. In our method of working, however, the deeper and more potent the energies and forms, the less outer verbal definition given to them.

This means in effect that if you attempt the deep stages of visualisation, those of the Four Gods, without working through the early stages of the Companions and the Goddesses, then you will find very little to work with. The appearance in power of the Four Gods comes as a result of working through the preceding sequence of visualisations; if you do so the gods will unquestionably appear, and you will be able to see, with your inner vision, your faculty of empowered imagination, their appearance quite clearly.

More important than their image or appearance is the unique character and feeling of each of the Four Gods and their Directions. The attributes of the Directions and of Sacred Space are shown in Figure 10, and these underpin the character of each of the four gods.

East

Dawn ,Spring, Element of Air, the Sword or Arrow, powers of Life. The Warrior god, mediator of life-giving and life-taking.

South

Noon, Summer, Element of Fire, the Rod or Staff or Spear, Powers of Light. The Priest-kings god, mediator of Light and Darkness.

West

Evening, Autumn, Element of Water, the Cup or Cauldron, powers of Love. The Poet's god, mediator of love and sacrifice.

North

Midnight, Winter, Element of Earth, the Shield or Mirror, powers of law and liberation. The Prophet's god, mediator of reason and madness.

Below

The power of the land and planet, ultimately the power of the Great Goddess of All Being.

Figure 10 - Sacred Space

Sacred Space is defined for us by the shape of a human being standing upon the surface of the land and planet. Seven Directions are aligned to: ABOVE/ BELOW/WITHIN/EAST/SOUTH/WEST/NORTH. The resulting sphere is infinite or contracted to the smallest imaginable location.

Above is the sky and stellar universe, below is the land. Within is our centre of existence, our primal and perfect Being.

The Four Directions of consciousness mirror the four planetary directions, defined for us by the magnetic fields of the Earth, and our orbit around the Sun. A further definition of stellar directions is through the movement of the Sun within the galaxy.

When we define awareness in Sacred Space, and align it to the Seven Directions, our energies and consciousness become increasingly balanced and enhanced. Sacred Space is alive with its own consciousness, and in meditation we find that Sacred Space responds and talks back to us, often in surprising ways.

In the manifest outer world all creatures occupy Sacred Space, and there is no such thing as 'inert matter'. In the Mysteries, Sacred Space is populated by ourselves, by gods and goddesses, and often by heroes, ancestors, and a wide range of other beings including companion creatures and non-human or non-organic entities. Many examples of this holism of beings occur in mythology, legend, and spiritual traditions.

Working within the Male Mysteries we limit the people in the Sacred Space to those who have the most powerful effect upon men in regular meditation, visualisation, and Sacred movement.

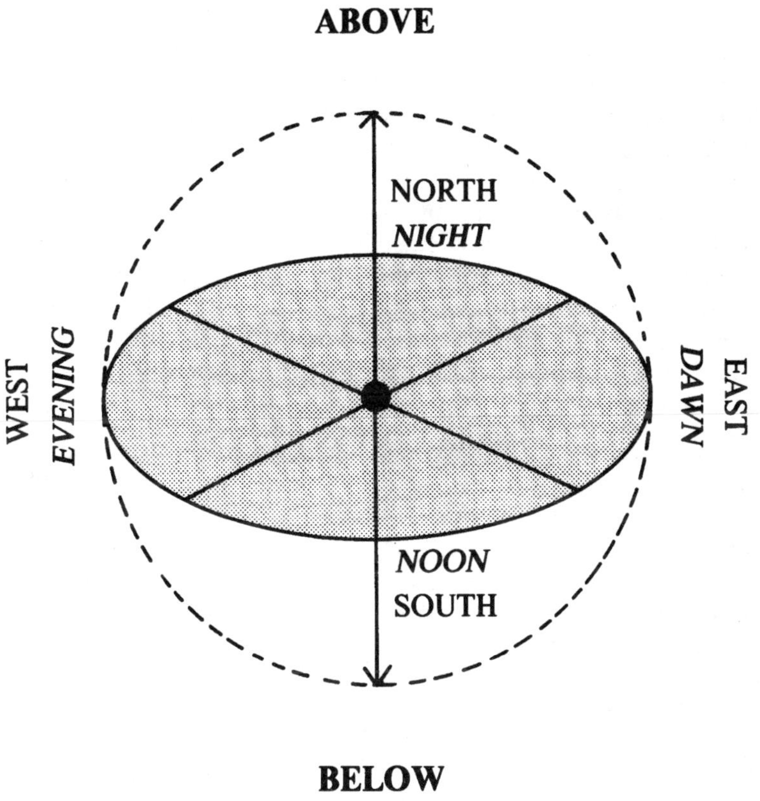
ABOVE
NORTH
NIGHT
WEST
EVENING
EAST
DAWN
NOON
SOUTH
BELOW

Above
The power of the stars, ultimately the power of the great God of All Being.

Remember that there is no religious requirement in these terms, no orthodoxy, paganism, or any other kind of -ism. These are simply the age-old, universal terms that humanity has used, concepts to partially define that which has no rigid definitions. All that you need to do is work through the sequences of visualisation, and with practice the entire structure of the Mystery comes alive. If you are later able to dispose of it altogether and work directly with energies that these primal images and patterns arouse, then you will have fulfilled part of your quest to know yourself. For most of us, however, certain patterns and archetypes or imaginal forms are essential as keys to empowerment. They act just as any material tool or vehicle or musical instrument, or other vital living aid to skill and motion and balance works - the form is theirs, the skill to work with it is ours, and eventually we become independent of the means or vehicles, even though we can and do use them regularly.

Encountering the Gods
You enter the second room, which is empty and still. The four doors are closed. In the centre of the room is a small circular altar or table, and you walk towards this. You stand with your palms resting upon the surface of this altar, and as you touch it the room seems to change shape and become a square, rotating until the four doors are located in new positions. One is before you in the East, one behind you in the West , one to your right in the South, and one to your left in the North. You meditate in silence upon the Four Directions, and wait for a door to open. *(Silent pause here.)*

Now the door in the East, directly before you opens, and a figure steps into its frame. He is the god of life-giving and life-taking, embodying the power of the perfect Warrior in all worlds. Look upon him and remember his appearance. *(Period of silent meditation here, allowing the image to take form.)*

Now the door in the West, behind you opens. You slowly step around the central alter, until you stand in the East, facing West. Framed in the doorway is a figure; he is the god of perfect love and immaculate death, embodying the power of the Poet in all worlds. Look upon him and remember his appearance. *(Period of silent meditation here, allowing the image to take form.)*

As you face West you feel the power of the god of the East

flow into you, until it seems you are the perfect Warrior looking upon the perfect Poet. Now you turn again and face East, and as you do so you feel the power of the god of the West flow into you, until it seems that you are the perfect Poet looking upon the perfect Warrior. You pause in communion with both gods, and their power harmonises and fills your being. *(Silent communion here.)*

Slowly the power of the god of the East and the god of the West fades, and the door before you closes. You turn around the central altar, and the door in the West closes. You feel the room move back to its familiar shape, and in the far corner you see a chair. You step six paces to this chair, and sit. Now you return to outer consciousness slowly, taking your time over the transition.

(Notes are made at this stage.)

You enter the second room, which is empty and still. The four doors are closed. In the centre of the room is a small circular altar or table, and you walk towards this. You stand with your palms resting upon the surface of this altar, and as you touch it the room seems to change shape and become a square, rotating until the four doors are located in new positions. One is before you in the East, one behind you in the West, one to your right in the South, and one to your left in the North. You meditate in silence upon the Four Directions, and wait for a door to open. *(Silent pause here.)*

You hear a door open on your left, and walk around the altar until you are facing North. A figure stands framed in the doorway: he is the god of madness and reason, embodying the power of the Prophet in all worlds.Look upon him and remember his appearance. *(Period of silent meditation here, allowing the image to take form.)*

Now you hear the door behind you in the South open. You step around the altar until you stand in the North facing south. A figure stands framed within the doorway, he is the god of light and darkness. Look upon him and remember his appearance. *(Period of silent meditation here, allowing the image to take form.)*

As you face the South, you feel the power of the god of the North flow into you until it seems that you are the perfect Prophet looking upon the perfect Priest. Now you step around the altar and stand in the South, facing North. You feel power of the god of the South flow into you, until you are the perfect Priest looking upon the perfect Prophet.

Now the power of both gods is harmonised and merged with you, and you commune with them in silence. *(Silent period for communion here.)*

Slowly the power of the god of the North and the god of the South fades, and the door before you closes. You turn around the central altar, and the door in the South closes. You feel the room move back to its familiar shape, and in the far corner you see a chair. You step six paces to this chair, and sit. Now you return to outer consciousness slowly, taking your time over the transition.
(Notes are made at this stage.)

You enter the second room, which is empty and still. The four doors are closed. In the centre of the room is a small circular altar or table, and you walk towards this. You stand with your palms resting upon the surface of this altar, and as you touch it the room seems to change shape and become a square, rotating until the four doors are located in new positions. One is before you in the East, one behind you in the West, one to your right in the South, and one to your left in the North. You meditate in silence upon the Four Directions, and wait for a door to open. *(Silent pause here.)*

The Four Doors open simultaneously, and you feel the presence of the gods of the Four Directions enter the room and flow into you, until they are perfectly balanced. *(Pause here.)*

Now you feel a deep movement in the ground beneath your feet, and the earth power rises up and out of the land to ascend your spine. It rises to your genitals, and you utter the word given to you by the goddess of the land; it rises to your heart and you are filled with boundless love; it rises to your throat and you breathe the universal breath; it rises to your head and your mind is filled with light. As the power rises into your head, you feel the presence of a responding power from above you, radiating down into your body. You pause in silent communion as the forces from Below and Above merge and harmonise within you, balanced and perfected by the gods of the Four Directions. *(Silent contemplation here.)*

Now you breath deeply, and acknowledge the gods of the Four Directions: in the East is the god of Warriors; in the West is the god of Poets; in the North is the god of Prophets; in the South is the god of Priests. In the depths is the power of the Great Mother, and in the Height the power of the Star Father.

In the centre is a man, yourself. Be at peace with yourself in silence. *(Pause here.)*

Now the power from Above and Below has merged within you, and it slowly fades, entering every part of your body becoming absorbed within your entire being. It gradually reduces in intensity yet remains dwelling in every part of you, even in your bones and in your blood and in your cells.

One by one the four gods withdraw, from the East, from the West, from the South from the North. You stand alone and complete within a calm empty room. Now the Fourfold room dissolves, and you return to your outer life, ready to mediate the power that you have experienced to all that lives.

11

Working Towards the Future of the Male Mysteries

The reader with a sense of humour might well observe that this book has progressively de-materialised. We began with chapters on the historical and psychological progress, or lack of progress, of men's inner disciplines, arts, and potentials in post-Christian materialist western culture. These arts and skills were then gradually redefined within a modern system incorporating many of techniques from the ancient imaginative arts, magical and spiritual traditions, and from the inner Mysteries themselves.

At this stage we began to move inwards, reaching beyond history and society, religion or psychology, into the seldom explored realms of energy and consciousness. The last stages of our visualisation programme, though simple, are extremely powerful. While having the most power, the last set of visualisations, those of the Four Gods, are also the briefest and least substantial or fully described of any in the book.

But after an inner resolution of energies, after finding some degree, however modest, of realisation, of unmasking, of kingship, what happens then? The answer must be that we seek to re-materialise the entire Mystery, to let the inherent power within flow out through men into the natural world, to be shared by all that lives.

There are a vast range of implications in terms of exercises and specific practices in this expression and sharing of the Mysteries. I hope to be able to explore and define these techniques in a further book, Volume Two. The most interesting implications are that, given a number of people who have worked through the entire sequence of empowering visualisations to some effect, this group might then work with other men towards sharing and expanding the changes of consciousness inherent in the Five Branches.

I have tried throughout this book to make such direct work a real possibility, removing the concepts of development and initiation from the old and decidedly rotten stereotype of the adept or master and pupil, or of the cunning all-knowledgeable therapist and wise man and the ignorant confused client or patient. These stereotypes must be broken and dissolved if we are to truly grow.

I should also state that I am not, at present, convinced that some of the more recently developed group techniques for men's awareness go far enough into the true male mystery to carry on forward into the future. We see typical examples in terms of group sharing of life-stories, sweat-lodges, learning to forgive our fathers, to redevelop male brotherhood and trust, and so forth. While I would not undervalue such methods, (particularly in the important context of developing trust and group sharing in a society which is designed to make men hostile to one another at all levels), they do not begin to approach the deeper energies and transformations inherent in all men. Perhaps they are not intended to do so.

In this last chapter, I would like to suggest, prior to the appearance of a full book on the subject, some of the techniques of group interaction possible in a modern redevelopment of the Male Mysteries. The foundation of this is, once again, found within the Four Branches. There are many transformative and therapeutic potentials in our simple structure of Companions, Goddesses, and Gods, working through methods of polarity and exchange of energies and ideas according to the basic patterns shown in the Mysteries - patterns which you, the reader, should by now have experienced to a greater or lesser extent by working with the visualisations in this book.

Working With Human Male Companions

For basic experiential group work, I would suggest that a group has no more than five members initially, but that after it has built some trust and companionship, this can be expanded by adding members until it becomes clearly too large to operate efficiently. The group then divides into further groups of five, and so forth. There are no leaders, teachers, or guides, other than those inner guides encountered through your increasing skill in visualisation.

So to begin, we simply need five men who have already worked individually with the visualisations, at least as far as the sequence of the Four Companions, and preferably through the entire cycle of Companions, Goddesses, and Gods, at least once.

As a group you will recognise a general affinity to a particular Branch within each of you: this is usually a fast and intuitive recognition. Intellectual argument or analytical dissection of character will only waste your time and energy. Besides, everyone in the group takes turns to work as a representative of each Branch, so no one is rigidly defined. We all have within us the Warrior, the Poet, the Prophet, the Priest, and the King. Some come to the fore during certain periods of a lifetime, others seem prominent in terms of established persona or character. Sometimes inner work will radically change us, so that a hitherto unconsidered Branch of the male energy and consciousness replaces our conditioned or self-deluded personality and its apparent link to a Branch or archetype.

Foundations of the Simple Group Method

The group method begins by choosing the Four Companions and one Worker. Once this basic choice has been made, the people simply rotate around the cycle, until you have all been a Worker, Warrior, Poet, Prophet, Priest, and of course King.

As a general rule, the group will arrange itself in the fourfold pattern of the Companions. The simple way to do this is to have a chair in each corner of your working room or space (not squarely in the Four Directions, but in the angles of such a square). The positions are shown in Figure 8.

The worker or primal man also sits, initially, at one end of the room, and all five Companions meditate and build the image of the Room with Four Doors, each door being behind or around, and framing, the man chosen during that particular session. This should be a very simple visualisation, with no long period of time or great effort involved.

The entire sequence of encountering the Branches one by one, and pair by pair, as described in Chapter 10 is then commenced. But now we encounter a male companion and trusted fellow worker, who mediates or represents the forces of the innerworld contact or archetype. The parts may be read aloud by each man on behalf of his own Branch, or may be worked from a recorded visualisation, such as those which accompany this book. When you reach later stages you do not, of course, literally throw each other through the wall, as occurs in the visualisation! Imagination is far more liberal than manifestation. If you have ever seen any ritual dancing in which a man is raised upon a platform of hands or swords, such ceremonies, found worldwide, are remnants, preserved in folklore, of the old Male Mysteries. The one who is raised is both king and worker, exalted and sacrificed. The modern counterpart is the visualisation where you pass through the mirror into the Second Room (page 129).

Simply working with the companions in turn, with a group of five men, will occupy a long cycle of experiences. There should be ample opportunities for discussion, noting reactions in all present, and comparing, eventually, how you emerge from the cycle to how you felt when you commenced it. When all five men have worked through the entire cycle, then is the time to form new groups of five, or to bring other men into the initial group.

In Conclusion

Obviously the foregoing methods are the merest indication of how we might proceed with group work and dramatic or ceremonial pattern making for men. The physical group does have an amplifying effect upon some of the subtle energies aroused in the visualisations, but I would stress that the key to balancing this is always by working with the goddess images, either as a group or individually. In the next book on the Mysteries I intend to show not only techniques for group work for men, but how the Male and Female Mysteries might formally and consciously work together in the twentieth and twenty-first centuries.

I would be pleased to read any reports on individual or group work with the visualisation programme given in this book. You may write to me care of the publisher, and if you enclose a stamped, self-addressed envelope (or an addressed envelope with an international postal coupon) I will do my best to respond. Please note that I cannot necessarily advise on personal life problems and that I do not presume or claim to give personal counselling, initiation or spiritual guidance.

R.J. Stewart
Bath, England

APPENDIX 1
APPROACHING SILENCE

There are a number of techniques for approaching Silence, used in both eastern and western spiritual disciplines or inner training. We shall concentrate upon one closely associated with western arts of transforming consciousness, as used throughout this book. The method is simple, and is based upon the concept of universal and individual spheres or fields of consciousness/energy/entity, and the Directions of East or Before, South or Right, West or Behind, North or Left, Above and Below. Your centre of being is the Seventh Direction, which is Within.

1. Sit in a relaxed upright position (upon a chair or upon the floor if you prefer). For this exercise the hands are usually laid in the lap, palm up, with the thumb-tips touching...some experiment will find a comfortable balanced location for the hands using this finger position, either with the back of the left hand over the right, or vice versa. The feet may be lightly crossed at the ankles: again right over left or left over right is found through your own intuition and preference, as it varies from individual to individual. If you adopt a floor sitting posture, the hand position remains the same, but the legs are usually crossed in the meditators or hunters posture, known around the world since ancient times. Complex yoga postures are not necessary, and should not be taken out of their proper spiritual and cultural context.

2. After a period of steady calming breathing, with eyes closed, a brief visualisation and definition of the Six Directions is made, as described in our earlier pages. This results in a generally attuned or orientated sphere or field of entity and energy: our self located within the room, the land, the planet, the universe, aligned according to the Directions and as balanced as possible.

3. We now seek to still customary inner activity (having already stilled outer activity). This is undertaken by inwardly reducing your sense of Time, Space, and Energy.

(a) Seek to suspend your sense of the passage of Time.
(b) Seek to suspend your sense of Space.
(c) Seek to still all Energies within and around you.

This technique acts upon your entire entity, and makes no separation between inner and outer conditions. The usual method is one of drawing inwards...as time is stilled, as space is withdrawn, and as energy ceases to interact, we pass deeper and deeper within towards our source of being. All that remains is quiet steady breathing, the breath of life itself.

4. Emerging from Silence involves drawing in a deep breath and exhaling it. This First Breath of air may then be uttered as Four Vowels[22], realigning the stilled sphere of being. We may also go no further than drawing the breath and returning to outer consciousness. With practice it is possible to reach through the three phases of Timelessness, Spacelessness and Poise (stilled energy) very rapidly.

To begin with however, the Approach to Silence requires patience and repeated simple practice. Strenuous effort will produce the opposite results to those required, and trick the mind into many side alleys of trivial interaction. The secret is to approach the stillness, the Silence, that is already within us, deep at the centre of our being. That silence is the state of un-being upon which our being is founded.

The approach to Silence creates relative conditions of stillness, peace, and poise. If we truly reached Silence we would pass into a state of existence that cannot be apprehended, for we would reach universal poise, perfect stillness. This condition, if such a word may be used, is found in various definitions in the world's mystical and religious teachings. In our present context, however, we merely seek to Approach Silence, and place no mystical or religious system upon this basic technique of realignment .

Appendix 2

Establishing an Innerworld Contact

The following exercise in visualisation is short; it may be undertaken regularly with increasing effect. No specific contact is named in our example, and the method may be used to clarify a number of contacts; with practice it leads to very deep and powerful levels of exchange and communication. Visualisation is primarily educational, in the true sense of the word, leading our consciousness out of its habitual grooves and fixations. Contacts developed through the imagination are invaluable to our general progress towards balance, regardless of any debate over the reality of the entities contacted. (See Chapter 3.)

1. Preparation

Sitting in the centre of your Circle, which is either a room, dedicated space, or your own body upon the chair, enter into visualisation. This is done by closing your eyes and imagining the pictures described, building them slowly and steadily. In guided visualisation, a script is read, recited or played back upon a tape recorder from a pre-recorded source.[14]

2. The Visualisation

Before you is a door; it is a plain wooden door set in a high stone wall. You look at this door in the wall for some time until it is utterly clear and solid; as you look you know that the instruction which you seek lies somewhere beyond the entrance that is sealed by the wooden door.

As you look, you realise that the door will not simply open on demand but only for someone with a valid reason for entry. You meditate upon your reason, clearly defining it in your awareness. In doing so, you inwardly recite a formula for passing through the entrance: 'I seek an innerworld contact to teach me the subject of...

I seek to pass within under the Light'. As you formulate this phrase, you see that a small lamp hangs over the door, with its flame glowing steadily. The door opens, and you rise and pass through the entrance.

You are in a small courtyard; it is square, surrounded by high stone walls. In the centre is a fountain bubbling from a circular basin. The courtyard floor is of flagstones, inscribed with faint designs. Against each of the four walls there grows a flowering tree, and below the branches of each tree, just to one side of the trunk, there is a door in each wall.

You walk into the centre of the courtyard, and move from left to right around the fountain, remembering your stated purpose for being admitted. You are waiting for a teacher or adviser to appear through one of the four doors where the blossoms fall. As you pace around the stone basin with its gentle trickle of water, you hear a door open and close quietly behind you. You turn, and place your hands upon the edge of the basin of the fountain. Standing opposite you is your teacher.

(At this point the effect of the visualisation will vary. Some people cannot see their innerworld contact immediately, and although the door always opens the contact sometimes remains out of sight, speaking while you continue to walk slowly around the fountain. Others may see their teacher immediately. It is very important to remember, and write down at a later time of recollection, the appearance of the contact; his or her face, clothing, any identifying objects or symbols, any suggestions of a name. Sometimes such details take a long time in coming forth; some contacts are reliable for years before you see an image or know a name. There is no need to try and force a contact to give you a 'name', providing you have a specific mode or symbol of identification.)

There is no further guided part to this visualisation, other than the simple closing pattern which is described below. For obvious reasons, the subject matter of the interaction between yourself and an innerworld being will vary infinitely, and only a general summary can be given of what might reasonably occur. After re-stating the subject matter chosen for education or enlightenment (though this is often unnecessary) you conduct a conversation with the contact. This is actually a type of mediation combined with images; in advanced stages the imagery fades into a more direct knowledge of the subject in hand.

In the initial stages, the subject matter should be carefully restricted and the time period kept short. Once you are attuned to a contact, a series of further inner experiences may be undertaken; the teacher may lead the student through a door, or present specific scenarios through the imagination. The student however, should not merely wander about willy-nilly, but keep to the matter in hand. If the contact is within established spiritual traditions, there will be little or no idle wandering allowed, and a drifting consciousness on the part of the individual will either break the contact or result in a reminder of the function and purpose of the meeting.

If in doubt about time duration, set an arbitrary period of comfortable length, say fifteen or twenty minutes, before starting the visualisation. Our inner clock will usually begin to withdraw the awareness at the time indicated...never use any mechanical means of interruption. The question of duration is subjective, and soon becomes a matter of individual or group style. A summary of the subject matter should be written out as soon as possible after withdrawing from the inner place, though experienced mediators may do so while retaining the inner contact in the imagination.

3. Closing the Contact

Now the communication is over, you are standing back in the courtyard, with your hands resting upon the bowl of the fountain. A door closes quietly behind you, and you realise that your innerworld contact has departed. You begin to walk slowly from left to right around the square courtyard; suddenly you feel prompted to stop in front of one of the flowering trees; you know intuitively that the door by this tree is the one that leads to your own outer world. There may be a symbol or object hanging from the lower-most branches; if there is, remember it, for it is a key to further experience in the innerworld, a key which may be used to pass to and fro easily. The door opens, and you see your room and chair beyond. You pass through, and hear the door close behind you. Slowly you merge back into the image of yourself seated in a room, facing the stone wall and the closed door. The image of the wall dissolves, and you open your eyes. All that remains is to close the Circle according to your custom.

4. Conclusion

Write out your experience, and if possible write a commentary upon the experience. This last is a very useful method, as much will come of a commentary that is not realised in the initial description or summary of the innerworld teaching and experience.

Appendix 3

Visualisation: The Guardian

In this expanded narrative for visualisation we seek to establish contact with one of the great primal god-forms, central to the Male Mysteries, and widely found in ancient Mysteries, magical arts, and religion. We should always be aware that the presence of a working image or method within an apparently outmoded ancient religion or formal tradition does not preclude its modern use. The mythic roots of each god- and goddess-form, or specific methods of transforming awareness, are far deeper than any formal presentation or cultural expression.

When we use images of this type to regenerate our inner energies, we are tapping into the mythic roots rather than any specific cult or historical or religious flowering of those roots. We are, in fact, slowly building a new branch of the Mysteries for the coming century.

The image of the Guardian is known worldwide in many variants, each variant having a fundamental identity and similar appearance to an archetypical Guardian. Local and historical expressions can and do take on specific forms and functions, and we need to be aware of the differences; indeed, the differences between expressions of an archetypical god- or goddess-form, ranging from universal to purely local, are important in direct work with images and energies.

There is a constant emphasis in modern spiritual or meditative teaching that we must realise the unity and uniformity of all such images and traditions, that they are all ultimately one. This may be true, but for us as humans the way begins with a clear understanding of one or two specific paths. These paths ultimately lead to unity, but we must travel the path first, and cannot reach unity by merely acknowledging it intellectually.

When we talk of the Guardian it should be emphasised that this is not simply an outmoded or redundant ancient god-form, but an enduring image inherent within human consciousness. For practical purposes it gives shape and entity as a living being to certain 'male' forces or energies, which we all, male and female, have within us. These energies, however, are not confined to any male, human, or imaginative, or transpersonal entity, or transformation of the psyche; they are also found in the environment, the land, the planet, the universe.

There is an individual or microcosmic reflection of any god-form, and a transpersonal or macrocosmic image. The greater image is not simply some type of vaguely universal god or goddess form, for it has an extremely potent and enduring presence within the collective consciousness of life forms. As far as we are concerned, this is essentially our collective ancestral consciousness, a realm of consciousness which is frequently used to great effect in the esoteric traditions of transformation and empowerment.

The forces embodied by the Guardian are also embodied by certain goddesses, but the gender of the image unquestionably alters and defines the manner in which it works, and its deep effect upon human beings. (In *The Merlin Tarot*[23] a pattern of polarity and octaves of power is found, broadly based upon the pan-cultural wisdom symbol of the Tree of Life. Tarot is often a good indicator of the inner and outer polarity of images, with male and female images alternating with every change of level or increasingly powerful card.)

In the classical world the Guardian god was known as Pan, the lord of nature, of the wild forces of growth, the creative energies that flow through all forms within the land. The wild energies of this god were said to be impossible to resist: his presence brought the fit of *panic* that is felt when potent energies are at work.

Modern fiction, based upon religious propaganda, has tended to brand this image as evil, licentious, savage, degenerate. The early Church fathers identified Pan as a false god, *deo falsus*, and eventually the Devil. This was simply because the sanctity of nature was regarded with suspicion by the Church. Nature was seen as a delusion or as a source of evil, for the elect were supposed to find their way to heaven as rapidly as possible, leaving the damned to burn in hell, and ignoring an abandoned earth far behind. This type of dualistic escapist elitism reappears, in subtle variants, in much of the current fashionable New Age literature and in related teachings. To emphasise light against or over darkness is one of the most corrupting and weakening concepts known to us; light and darkness exist in a rhythm together, and humans, like plants and simpler life forms, require the cycle of light and darkness to grow and change. Excessive light or darkness, periods of either that are too long or too short, lead to imbalance. If we extend this analogy or resonance to plant growth a little further, we might liken the Mysteries and the perennial techniques of transformation to a deep understanding and practical application of the secret rhythms of nature.

On an inner level, the god Pan represents not only wild vital forces, but the herdsman or controller of such forces. It is through his power that we both grow and learn to give form to growth, to drive and tame our energies according to a set of natural simple laws. Thus he is also a god of taking, of limitation. The Mysteries of Pan, and of his Celtic counterpart Cernunnos, to whom we shall turn shortly, were particularly loathed by the orthodox Church, as they represented a way of spiritual liberation through natural energies, and were closely linked to the ancient all-pervasive worship of the Great Mother. The Herdsman, Guardian, or Green Man, is the wild son of the great Mother.

The Horned God, known to the Celts as Cernunnos was widespread in the ancient world; versions of his image are found in prehistoric cave paintings, and as far west as America among the gods of the native people. He was Guardian of the Mysteries of the Underworld, sometimes shown (as in Romano-Celtic images from the first century BC) sitting upon or close to a hoard of coins, gold, or precious metal work. He held serpents in either hand, and was often identified with the fruits of the earth, both in the form of animals and growing plants. One of the most famous representations of this god is found in the silver Gundestrup Cauldron, dating from the 2nd century BC. The narrative sequence of pictures upon the cauldron are typical to the Male Mysteries and their relationship to the great Mystery of life, death, and rebirth.[17]

Thus we might summarise this deity, embodying for us as a set or pattern of energies, as the Keeper, the Protector, and the refiner of forces into beneficial form. No beneficial growth or form can occur without limitation, purification, and selection. So he is also a god of taking, of challenge. In human terms he is one of the Guardians of thresholds of consciousness and energy: he prevents us from accessing more energy than we may truly cope with, yet if we are able to pass through his strict tests, controls and therapeutic inner transformations, he gives us free entry to the realms of power, symbolised by the mysterious Underworld, but manifesting as form in nature.

Other guardians arise within consciousness due to individual circumstances, and yet other guardians are known upon collective levels, and in specific locations. But as far as humanity is concerned, the Guardian is generally the pervasive image of a horned man. While awareness of this image and its potential has been suppressed in our culture for several centuries, it returns now, inevitably, as we awaken to the destruction and pollution of nature...by which we include ourselves as both aggressors and victims of such madness. The Guardian was, and is, one of the major controls of such madness, leading the wild energies into proper paths. Due to our removal of this image, and related Goddess images, from our lives, we have run riot over the land, the planet. The terrible results are now becoming only too clear, the results of excessive forced growth in artificial light, with no recuperative empowering darkness.

Meeting the Guardian

The individual or group spends a preparatory period in silence, using the meditation of Stillness (page 146) or a similar calming, clearing technique. As always with such preparatory stages, the emphasis must be upon stillness and silence, and not on any specific image, divine or meditative form, or religious meditational technique. The aim of this period of stillness is to calm all energies/thoughts/emotions and so become ready for a clear, uncorrupted or undistracted image to be built and to work within the imagination.

First we visualise a forest: tall trees and primal untouched woodland growth. The great trees rise up to the sunlit sky above, filtering the light through their huge canopy of branches, until it falls in green and golden shafts and pools upon the rich carpet of deep loam and mosses below. This is an ancient oak forest, and many of the trees have wide gnarled trunks showing great age.

Gradually we enter into this forest, and feel the presence of the trees, emanating an intense radiant force like warmth all round us. We hear birds calling, and the wind constantly stirs the leaves and higher branches, making a flowing ceaseless sound like the rippling of water, the tides of the sea. As we walk deeper into the forest, we find a narrow deer trail, and follow this through the trees to a clearing. The clearing is small, with a huge ancient wide-trunked oak tree in the centre, growing out of a pile of jumbled rocks. From a cleft in the rocks, a tiny spring flows, making a damp pool of lush green growth. We see that the rocks are red, and that there are tracks of many animals coming to this central spring, to drink the water, and lick the salt. In this clearing we pause, and wait in silence, knowing that we seek the presence of the Guardian.

(Here a silent pause is made in the narrative or guided visualisation. The length of time depends upon the individual or group. For individual work this is usually a brief period, but for guided work with groups it may be lengthened.)

As we meditate we realise that we have been joined by someone. From behind the tree a man has emerged, who looks steadily upon us as if in calm unhurried judgement. He is a teacher and guide in the Male Mysteries, and is willing to take us into the presence of the Guardian if we truly seek to do so. With this man there is an animal, keeping him close company. Look upon the animal and remember it.

Our guide beckons us towards the spring rising from the rocks, and shows us a small scarred rough stone bowl by the side of the water. He fills this with water and splashes some water into our faces, as if in lustration and preparation. The water is ice-cold and shocks us wide-awake. Even as we wipe the water from our eyes, we see that our guide has moved behind the tree, and we hurry to follow him.

As we pass to the other side of the tree, we seem to step from light to darkness, day to night. Ahead of us we see the guide and his animal passing swiftly over a bare star-lit plain; the trees of the forest have disappeared, and the ground is hard and cold. We realise that we are running now, and that we must breathe deeply to keep up with our guide and his companion animal. The cold air fills our lungs and we breath in and out deeply, seeming to gain speed with very breath. The effort is hard at first, but gradually brings with it a deep rhythm that gives us increasing strength and speed.

Far ahead of us we see a glimmer of light, as if the sun is beginning to rise: as we settle into the rhythm of running and breathing, we realise that the plain is not empty, as we had first thought. Occasionally on either side, we see the dim shapes of other creatures moving in the starlight. Sometimes they approach, as if curious, while others flee at our coming. Some of the shapes are vast, and we uneasily recognise creatures from other times and places, creatures which we fear. Yet the speed and rhythm of our running is moving us swiftly ahead, following our guide and his animal: their presence seems to deter anything from being too curious or coming too close.

Now we find that it is growing light, and we come to the end of the bare plain. Our guide slows his pace and pauses to wait for us to approach. We find that we are once again on the edge of a forest, and as the sun rises a dawn chorus of many birds rises to the light. But this forest is of trees and plants that we have never seen: the trees have a smooth glossy green and red bark, rising to a vast height, and the leaves far above shed a deep blue and purple light, filtering the sun as it rises. The crying birds lift a vast chorus of calls and whistles, which is joined by the roaring of great beasts, and the screaming of small animals in the huge branches above. As we ran across the plain we felt like warriors at the chase, but now we feel small, like children, dwarfed by the tall trees, and the presence of such seething roaring life.

Our guide briefly touches the animal that accompanies him, and they step aside to reveal a entrance leading into the earth at the foot of two huge trees. The thick smooth roots of these trees tangle together, forming a low arch, and our guide indicates that we must pass within. We feel the growing heat and light of the day, and the air is moist and filled with powerful scents. Within those shadowy roots seems to be a resting place, a shelter from the primal forest, and we slowly stoop to pass within.

We find ourselves in a low earthen passageway, which leads gently downwards. It is of hard compacted soil, and bears the marks of many passing hooves and claws; suddenly we are less certain about this place. Our guide and his companion animal have remained above, and we move slowly downwards alone. The tunnel widens out into a large chamber, which has a strong animal smell as if many beasts have sheltered here. The far of end of this chamber is lit by tiny lamps burning with a dim yellow flame: a raised platform of fresh green branches is laid there, and we smell strong resins and sharp bitter herbs, cutting through the primal odour. As we look upon this platform, we feel a deep uncontrollable fear rise within us, making our hair stand on end, and our skin shiver. We realise that we are in the presence of the Guardian, and his power brings us to the edge of panic.

Set far back in the shadows, where the light of the lamps barely touches, we realise that a figure is sitting cross-legged upon the green branches. His face is hidden from us, but we see strong sinewy arms and legs, covered in deep spiralling tattoos. The flickering lamp-light first reveals and then conceals these patterns, which seem to writhe like snakes upon his dark skin. We realise that he has long hair and a beard, and that a tall crown of spreading antlers is upon his head. His eyes are in shadow, and we are, for the moment, relieved that he does not look fully upon us in the light. Slowly, uncertainly, we sit, and gradually calm ourselves, waiting in the presence of the Guardian.

(Here a silent period is spent: this should be as long as possible. As a general rule, this level of visualisation can be brief, but with practice it may be lengthened.)

As we sit we gain many realisations concerning the Guardian: what he conceals, what he reveals, how he may keep us from passing where we might destroy ourselves, and how he may prevent us from destroying that which we do not understand. In the lamp light his face is slowly revealed to those that dare to look upon him. He sits still, unmoving, unmoved by our presence, yet we feel a huge vigour and power flowing out from him; it encompasses us, enters into us, and triggers energies within our selves which have never known before. *(A brief silence here.)*

As we sit in that underground chamber, we slowly realise that the scent in the warm air is changing. At first it was the odour of many animals, seeming to come from the earth itself. Then the resinous and sharp smell of herbs and healing plants rises from the leafy platform at the end of the chamber; now this astringent smell is replaced by that of flowers. Faint at first, then with increasing presence, we smell the perfume of many different flowers, as if the blooms from a rich wild garden from a fertile land have been scattered all around us.

As this complex and delicate sequence of perfumes grows stronger, we realise that a figure is standing at the edge of the raised platform. In the lamp light we see that this is a beautiful young woman with long flowing hair; she wears a simple robe woven with a pattern of plants and flowers. The figure of the Guardian has receded into deepest shadow, though we know that he remains seated on the platform. The lamplight reflects from the brilliant colour of the young woman's dress, revealing first one plant, then another, then scenes and images, woven in and out of the flowers, hidden deep within the pattern of the fabric.

We look upon her long golden hair and cornflower blue eyes,

and feel that her presence lifts many shadows from our hearts, our personal shadows that the Guardian had drawn up from deep within us. The young woman steps across the chamber, and as she moves the perfume of flowers grows intense; the sound of her robe is like the rustling of a great garden in early morning wind. As the entrance way, she lifts her hand, and we see that she holds a small living branch, with fresh green leaves, buds, and opening flowers. We pause to look upon her standing et the doorway. *(Here a short silent pause is made.)*

Now the young woman beckons to us, and we follow her through the tunnel and up the sloping way towards the surface. We emerge into red sunlight, shining directly into our eyes, making them water. Even as we recover our sight, we realise that the woman has vanished, and that we stand back at the original clearing in the first oak forest, in the light of sunset. We have emerged where we began , coming from a passageway concealed within the roots of the oak tree, out through the rocks which also release the tiny spring into the glade.

In the trees we can see the movement of many animals, making their way through the woods, and we hear the evening song of birds. The forest is filled with a sense of restfulness and peace. *(Here a brief pause is made.)*

We realise that our guide and his companion animal wait at the edge of the glade, and know that we must travel with them down the narrow deer trail through he trees. As they lead us out of the forest, the sun truly sets, casting long shadows through the trees. At the very forest edge, our guide bids us sit and rest. Once again the great sense of peace that fills the land at sunset washes through us, and we close our eyes to sit in silence at the threshold of day and night. *(Take a short pause here.)*

Gradually the sounds and scents of the oak forest fade away, and we quietly return our outer world: in our inner vision the trees dissolve, and we feel the springy grass beneath us become the surface of a chair. We slowly open our eyes, and return to a familiar room. Our meeting with the Guardian and with the Maiden is over.

(Notes may be made at this point, or a discussion if required. It is important that people are not forced in any way to share their experience, and no demands should be made upon anyone unwilling to describe their experiences.)

Bibliography

The following list of books is not a definitive study course or exhaustive reference list. Many of the books listed here contain detailed Bibliographies for further study if required.

(Numbers refer to notes in main text.)

1. Stewart, R.J.
(a) *The Way of Merlin*, Unwin Hyman, London 1991.
(b) *The Prophetic Vision of Merlin*, Penguin, Arkana, London 1986.
(c) *The Mystic Life of Merlin*, Penguin, Arkana, London 1987.
(d) *The Merlin Tarot*, Book and full colour deck of cards (artwork by Miranda Gray), Aquarian Press, Wellingborough 1988.
(e) *The Book of Merlin* (editor), Blandford Press, London 1988.
(f) *Merlin and Woman* (editor), Blandford Press, London 1988. Also:Tolstoy, N. *The Quest for Merlin*, Hamish Hamilton, London 1985.

2. Graves, R.
(a) *The White Goddess*, Faber and Faber, London, 1975.
(b) *The Greek Myths*, Penguin, Harmondsworth (2 vols) 1965.
Also: Cumont, F. *Oriental Religions in Roman Paganism*, Dover, New York 1955.

3.Sjöö, M & Mor, B. *The Great Cosmic Mother*, Harper and Row, San Francisco 1987.
Gimbutas, M. *The Language of the Goddess*, Harper and Row, San Francisco 1989.
Stone, M. *When God was a Woman*, Dial Press 1976.

4. Stewart, R.J.
(a) *Music and the Elemental Psyche*, Aquarian Press, Wellingborough 1985.
(b) *Music, Power, Harmony*, Blandford Press, London 1990. Also: Berendt, Joachim-Ernst, *The Third Ear*, Element Books, Shaftesbury 1987.

5. Bolen, J.S. *Gods in Everyman*, Harper and Row, San Francisco 1989.
Jung, C.G. (a) *Archetypes of the Collective Unconsciousness* and *The Concept of the Collective Unconscious* in *Collected Works*, Vol. 9, Part 1, Princeton University Press 1968.
(b) *Man and His Symbols* (ed) Aldus, London 1979.

6. See 1 (d) for cosmology and psychology of tarot, chess, and similar pattern-making 'games'.

7. Stewart, R.J. & Matthews, J. *Celtic Battle Heroes*, Firebird Books, Poole 1988.

8. Plato, *The Republic* (various translations and editions).

9. Matthews, C. *Arthur and the Sovereignty of Britain*, Penguin, Arkana, London 1987.

10. Stewart, R.J. *The Underworld Initiation*, Aquarian Press, Wellingborough 1983. (Two further books on Underworld traditions forthcoming, to be published by Element Books, Shaftesbury 1991 and 1992).

11.Knight, G, (in) *Psychology and the Spiritual Traditions* (ed) R.J.Stewart, Element Books, Shaftesbury 1990.

12. Stewart, R.J.
(a) *The Elements of Creation Myth*, Element Books, Shaftesbury 1989.
(b) *The Elements of Prophecy*, Element Books, Shaftesbury, 1989.

13. See 1 (d) above.

14. Cassette tapes of the visualisations in this book, read by the author, with original music, are available from: Sulis Music, BCM 3721, London WC1N 3XX.

15. Stewart, R.J.
(a) *Living Magical Arts*, Blandford Press, Poole 1987.
(b) *Advanced Magical Arts*, Element Books, Shaftesbury 1988.
(c) *Psychology and the Spiritual Traditions* (ed) Element Books, Shaftesbury 1990.

16. Stewart, R.J. *Where is St George?*, Moonraker Press, Bradford on Avon, 1977, Humanities Press, New Jersey, USA 1978, Blandford Press, London 1989.

17. Stewart R.J. *Celtic Gods and Goddesses*, Illustrated by Miranda Gray and Courtney Davis, Photographs by Tim Cann. Blandford Press 1990.

18. Stewart, R.J. & Matthews, J. *Warriors of Arthur*, Blandford Press 1988.

19. See 2(b), also King, William (1710) *An Historical Account of the Heathen Gods and Heroes*, reprinted with introduction by Ross Nichols, Centaur Press, London 1965.

20. Ibid, also 17 above.

21. See 12 (b) above.

22. See 4 (b) above.

23. See 1 (d) above.

Further Reading

Angus, S. *The Mystery Religions and Christianity*, John Murray, London 1925.

Eliade, M.(a) *From Primitives to Zen*, Collins, London 1977.
(b) *Shamanism*, New York 1964.

Humphreys, C. *Concentration and Meditation*, Watkins, London 1959.

MacCana, P. *Celtic Mythology*, Hamlyn, London 1975.

Matthews, J. *The Choirs of the God* (ed) Unwin Hyman, London 1991.

Oesterly, W.O.E. & Robinson, T.H. *Hebrew Religion, Its Origin and Development*, SPCK, London 1940.

Steinbrecher, E. *The Inner Guide Meditation*, Aquarian Press, Wellingborough, 1988.

Wilhelm, R. and Jung, C.G. *The Secret of the Golden Flower*, Routledge & Kegan Paul, 1972.

Wind, E. *Pagan Mysteries in the Renaissance*, Oxford University Press, Oxford 1980.

INDEX